Design
Yourself!

Design Yourself!

Kurt Hanks / Larry Belliston / Dave Edwards

CRISP PUBLICATIONS, INC.

Dedicated to Corinne, Marjorie and
Jennifer, our wives. Thanks for being
understanding through this ordeal.

Library of Congress Catalog Card Number: 76-56620

ISBN 1-56052-046-9

Contents

What's it all about?

When you buy a tool or appliance the manufacturer usually includes instructions for its use. Rarely would you expect to need directions on how to read a book. **DESIGN YOURSELF** is not just a book; actually it is more like a special visual device with which you can examine your relationship to design and your role as a designer.

Educational books usually have a style that is authoritative—the reader is expected to respond to the book as facts written in stone not to be changed. With this book the burden of responsibility lies with the reader, for design is more dynamic than most subjects. Its goal, unlike that of many other books, is not only to increase the reader's knowledge but to encourage action. With this book, mastering the concepts is the first step, but the crucial goal is to apply them to a meaningful end within your own life.

Because good design is to a degree interpretation (making what you see, hear, read or feel mean something to you) we offer the warning that despite the authoritative sound which accompanies anything in print— including this book— you must filter and evaluate what you read. What you like in the book, remember and use; what you don't like, forget.

For those whose design ability is highly developed, this book should be like a dessert; for those whose ability is not yet fully blossomed, the book should be an appetizer that will encourage exploration of tantalizing areas.

Just reading this book is like clapping with one hand—to be most effective it must have your full participation. You can talk to this book, play with it, forget it or make it serve your needs! You can argue with this book because it does not hesitate to express definite opinions. The materials here are to be treated not as indisputable facts but as ideas to evaluate. Try them on for size, shake them up, roll them around and make them mean something to you—make them serve you.

The book is a little bit of everything in the way of ideas, games, puzzles, experiences and exercises and much of what it says depends upon your feelings, your interpretation, present and past experiences and what you will do about it all.

This book contains exciting, fun, invigorating, new, motivating information that should be a draft of fresh air in a sometimes polluted

WARNING: The authors of this book believe that a lackadasical design attitude will be dangerous to your HEALTH.

1

educational environment. We hope it will be fun, rewarding and a valuable tool as you set about designing in your own life. But to be useful a tool must be used.

You can relax with this book, but if you are one who prefers not to get involved, then set the book down now. **DESIGN YOURSELF** was created to help you feel better in your environment as a designer because it will mean more to you, as you put yourself "into" that environment by understanding and becoming involved.

What is Design ?

Design is an elusive concept. Depending on who is defining it and the context in which it is used, design can mean many different things.

Design is one of the most important factors of our lives, but often one of the most neglected. If a person does not design he is at least ruled by the designs of others. The following is a chart of circumstances or principles which relate you to design. Mark an X in the box by each item where you picture yourself as the designer.

- [ ] **Selecting the clothes you wear**
- [ ] **Buying or building a new home**
- [ ] **Drawing or doodling**
- [ ] **Customizing a car**
- [ ] **Modifying a dress or making clothes**
- [ ] **Choosing the music you listen to**
- [ ] **Choosing furniture**
- [ ] **Styling your hair**
- [ ] **Tattoo of a heart on your chest**
- [ ] **Arranging your bedroom**
- [ ] **Whistling a new tune**
- [ ] **Losing a scholarship by not applying**
- [ ] **Making posters or decorating for a social**
- [ ] **Kissing that super-looking last date**
- [ ] **Wishing you had bought that new coat**

As you can see, design is many things in many circumstances. Your whole day is governed by design at least to a certain degree.

After completing the exercise you must agree that YOU ARE A DESIGNER! You may not think you are able to draw, but you are a designer. You may not carve pieces of sculpture, but you are still a designer because you use the principles of design many times throughout your daily life. You arrange your room in a way that works well; you select clothing that makes you look good and feel comfortable; you live each day the best you know how; YOU ARE A DESIGNER whether you know it or not.

One way to look at it is that you design every day of your life. During each day you decide whether to **OPTIMIZE** and make the most of that day. If you don't willfully consider each day then you are designing by neglect. The principles which you will use as a designer are the same ones you can use to regulate your life productively. Even though you may have no intention of becoming a professional designer, this book could prove to be an invaluable tool in your life. Don't stop now . . .you may find the things to come both **FUN** and **REWARDING!**

DESIGN IS FINDING THE OPTIMUM IN A PARTICULAR SET OF CIRCUMSTANCES.

4

Good design is finding the best solution to a problem, given certain guidelines or limitations within which to work. An example might be that as a clothes designer you are asked to create a wardrobe for a fat lady. Since your design is for a fat person, you must work within the limitations given in order to produce a successful and acceptable design. A good designer will **OPTIMIZE** the situation by finding the very best solution to a problem within the given limitations which confront him.

Design is also governed by what could be called the "It depends rule." A beautiful flowing nightgown for Mary may not be a good design for Alfred who likes to wear Winnie the Pooh pajamas. What was good design yesterday may not be good design today. What is good design today may not be good design tomorrow. Most certainly there are principles which help one evaluate good design, but there are no rules which may not be broken to produce a better result under certain conditions.

The horizontal lines make the lady on the left look wider. The same woman looks thinner, as a result of vertical emphasis, as pictured on the right.

Assuming that automobiles in the past were the best designed cars, then the mere fact that gasoline is not as available today makes yesterday's cars poorly designed by today's standards. Take Volkswagen for example. For many years it had very little change. It sold well, was popular, got good gas mileage and was generally accepted as a good buy. But people's attitudes changed and so did the popular "Beetle." The comfortable little car became more comfortable by better utilizing space and providing more leg room for the occupants. The economical little car became more economical. And even the standard popular "Beetle" look gave way to a more "pleasing" design.

Making things "look nice" is only one isolated principle of good design. Simplicity, appropriate form, function and economics are examples of other important design principles.

Look for the mechanics of the mental processes as you devour the ensuing pages. Design might be a much more rewarding mental experience than you had imagined.

DRAWING

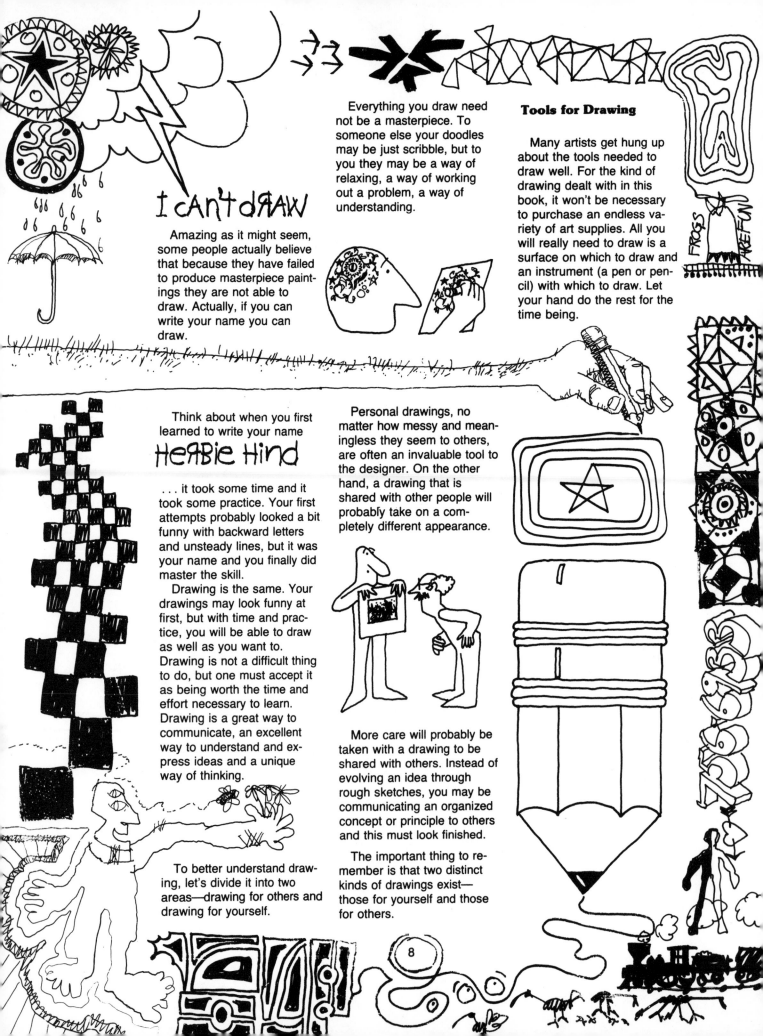

I cAn't dRAW

Amazing as it might seem, some people actually believe that because they have failed to produce masterpiece paintings they are not able to draw. Actually, if you can write your name you can draw.

Everything you draw need not be a masterpiece. To someone else your doodles may be just scribble, but to you they may be a way of relaxing, a way of working out a problem, a way of understanding.

Tools for Drawing

Many artists get hung up about the tools needed to draw well. For the kind of drawing dealt with in this book, it won't be necessary to purchase an endless variety of art supplies. All you will really need to draw is a surface on which to draw and an instrument (a pen or pencil) with which to draw. Let your hand do the rest for the time being.

Think about when you first learned to write your name

HeRBie Hind

. . . it took some time and it took some practice. Your first attempts probably looked a bit funny with backward letters and unsteady lines, but it was your name and you finally did master the skill.

Drawing is the same. Your drawings may look funny at first, but with time and practice, you will be able to draw as well as you want to. Drawing is not a difficult thing to do, but one must accept it as being worth the time and effort necessary to learn. Drawing is a great way to communicate, an excellent way to understand and express ideas and a unique way of thinking.

To better understand drawing, let's divide it into two areas—drawing for others and drawing for yourself.

Personal drawings, no matter how messy and meaningless they seem to others, are often an invaluable tool to the designer. On the other hand, a drawing that is shared with other people will probably take on a completely different appearance.

More care will probably be taken with a drawing to be shared with others. Instead of evolving an idea through rough sketches, you may be communicating an organized concept or principle to others and this must look finished.

The important thing to remember is that two distinct kinds of drawings exist—those for yourself and those for others.

Try Your Hand at Doodling

Copy

No No No

Have you ever heard that "COPYING IS A NO NO." You could probably learn to draw if shut up in a closet, but think of the time it would take. You can learn a drawing technique from others in minutes whereas it might take years to learn on your own.

Without access and the ability to learn from others even the very simple skills would be incredibly hard to learn. Ralph Waldo Emerson once said that if you isolated a man and didn't allow him to interact with his surroundings you would destroy him. He said, "The world exists for the education of each man."

All of the great masters learned the value of copying and studying the technique of accomplished artists. Di Vinci and Michelangelo worked as apprentices in art studios for years before their genius developed to the point where they could stand alone.

A man once said, "There is no need or time for my son to relearn by experience that which I have already learned. He should not start from the ground, but from my shoulders."

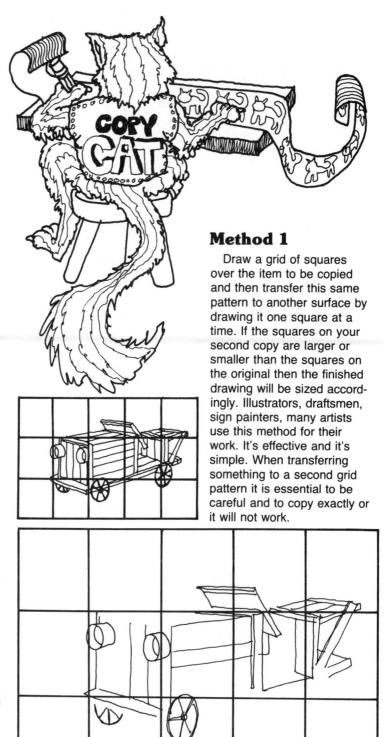

Method 1

Draw a grid of squares over the item to be copied and then transfer this same pattern to another surface by drawing it one square at a time. If the squares on your second copy are larger or smaller than the squares on the original then the finished drawing will be sized accordingly. Illustrators, draftsmen, sign painters, many artists use this method for their work. It's effective and it's simple. When transferring something to a second grid pattern it is essential to be careful and to copy exactly or it will not work.

Method 2

How many times have you drawn something and erased and redrawn, over and over again? Have you ever thought of using tissue to evolve a drawing? When you get something that looks pretty good but isn't quite there, try tracing it keeping the good parts and leaving the bad parts. This is an easy way to simplify or make a drawing more complex.

Tracing is an excellent way to determine placement for good design. By using this method you will most likely end up with a cleaner copy and a better solution to your drawing. You'll find that for the most part copying with a tissue is faster than belaboring a single sheet.

Method 3

One of the best and a more advanced form of copying is tracing nature. Take a piece of glass, hold it securely in front of you. Trace with

Have the drawing evolve, with the best drawing and design floating to the top sheet.

a felt pen whatever object lies behind the glass.

After having done this a few times you'll begin to understand the principle of true drawing which is simply transferring the image of an object to a linear form on a flat surface. That's all drawing on an opaque surface (such as paper) is—just tracing by transferring what you see to the surface before you. The only difference between using glass and an

opaque surface is that the clear surface you hold BE-TWEEN you and the object while the opaque surface you don't hold directly between you.

Learn by copying but don't become so dependent upon it that you use it as a crutch.

Copy From Nature

SIZE

One of the first principles of drawing we learn is SIZE; the closer things are the larger things look. Look at the top circles at the top of the page. Doesn't the largest circle at the top of the page look closer?

Big is close—small is far away

For the most part, drawing is the ability to create the illusion of depth and dimension.

When a new baby first begins to see things clearly you may have noticed that he flinches when objects move in front of him. He has no concept of where the objects are in relation to himself. As time goes on he begins to realize when things are close or far away. One of the things he learns is that an object of a standard size—such as a person—seems larger when it is closer to him and smaller when it is farther away.

Let's refer to the creature from the black lagoon to see how the different size relationships tell you that his foot and hand are closer to you. His front foot is bigger and therefore closer to you than his other foot. His hand appears to be larger than his head, although his head is actually probably larger than his hands, and this tells you that his hand is closer to you. Without the other parts of his body to compare his foot and hand to, you would not be able to recognize depth at all. In other words, size only creates the illusion of depth if an object of a known size is available for comparison.

12

Our mind automatically judges size for us. If we take a square and draw it in relationship to objects of known size with which we are familiar, it becomes obvious how our mind creates depth. In all of the next few illustrations a rectangle is shown.

A person leaning against a box tells us that it is about the size of an office desk.

As you can see, size is relative. We know the size of something by comparing it to other things. Without comparisons in natural settings, size, depth and dimensions would be difficult to determine. Without objects for comparison in drawings, size and depth would be virtually impossible to demonstrate.

You will notice in the first picture that the box is quite large. It could be a garbage dump or a crate with some large equipment inside.

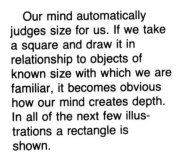

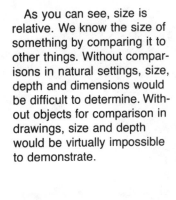

Now it has become a building with people scurrying around.

Someone standing on the box shape indicates that it is about the size of a building brick.

A Volkswagen parked in front of the rectangle places its size as that of a double garage door. In fact, it probably is a garage door.

Inside is a white wall, but we feel uncomfortable. We can't determine the size of the wall because there is nothing to compare it to.

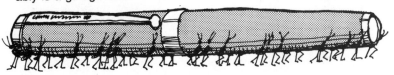

Detail

Thou shalt always remember that the closer things are to the viewer the more detail can be seen. Remember that detail is used in drawing to add emphasis.

Detail repeated over and over again becomes a pattern.

Look closely at the things around you. The closer things are to you the better you can see them and the more detail you can distinguish. This obvious natural occurance is used in drawing to help create the illusion of reality in the objects drawn. If you pick out certain objects which are close to the viewer in a drawing and give them slightly more detail then the rest of the drawing it will help to add flavor. When this is not done drawings can look 'washed out' and lack the 'pizzaz' necessary to make them come to life.

To emphasize a portion of a drawing a contrast of some sort is used. In the case of detail, more detail in a certain portion of a drawing draws attention to this area if the rest of the drawing lacks detail. At the same time, if a drawing has a great deal of detail then a portion in the drawing which lacks detail will be dominant.

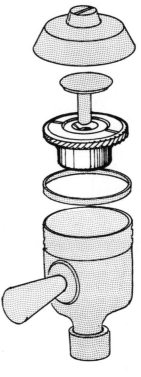

The use of detail is especially useful for construction drawings, working drawings, technical drawings and mechanical drawings. The example above shows how detail emphasizes and simplifies the technical aspects of this rendering.

"Probably the very most important concept to remember about de-tail is de-head. Quite often artists get de-head mixed up with de-tail and they lose sight of reality."

Don Keyy

Detail is used in the composition of a drawing to add emphasis. The drawing above is an example of the use of detail to draw attention to certain parts in the drawing. The flowers in the lady's hat attract attention. The busy-ness of the flowers contrasted with the simplicity of the lady emphasize the hat.

The detail in the hat also exemplifies the fact that detail creates a pattern.

Detail serves best to contrast when lack of detail dominates the rest of a drawing. If detail were used throughout a drawing then it would form a monotonous pattern and would lack emphasis.

Overlapping

Overlapping gives scale, depth, unity and interest

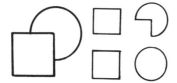

Look at the illustration of two geometric forms. . .what do you see? Is it a picture of a square in front of a circle or is it a square and a circle with a cut out portion? Your first impression was probably that the forms were of a square in front of a circle. Experience tells us that objects in front of each other overlap and block out parts of the object behind.

Ths objects shown below don't relate easily. It is difficult to know their relative sizes and positions.

The overlapping of items in a drawing gives relationship, a more comfortable feeling, direction, and dimension to the individual component parts of the drawing.

Overlapping creates the illusion of depth

When the items are separated it is hard to tell if they really relate or are individual items haphazardly arranged in a composite drawing.

Depth

Overlapping creates the illusion of depth. It tells us which item is closer or which is farther away. It lets us know the relative position of things.

Unity

Settings or drawings hold together better if items overlap. Things seem to relate to one another more comfortably if they appear to overlap. Individual items in a drawing are too loose and free. When overlapped, however, the drawing begins to hold together and become a unified working piece. Notice in nature around you that overlapping seems to unify the surroundings. Most good art overlaps and groups things to give direction and unity within the composition.

Scale

Scale, or relative size of objects is made more obvious by overlapping. If two items appear to be the same size, but one is obviously well in front of the other, then you know that the back item must be larger.

Interest

Overlapping gives interest to drawings. Composition and direction in drawings very often depend upon overlapping to create the illusion. The better the composition, the more intriguing the direction, the better the drawing. Items that lay on top of, wrap around, or lean against something are generally more interesting to look at. Overlapping creates a curiosity factor also—it makes you wonder what the part is like that you can't see!

We live in a "thing in front of thing world." Everything has a place in front of or behind another object.

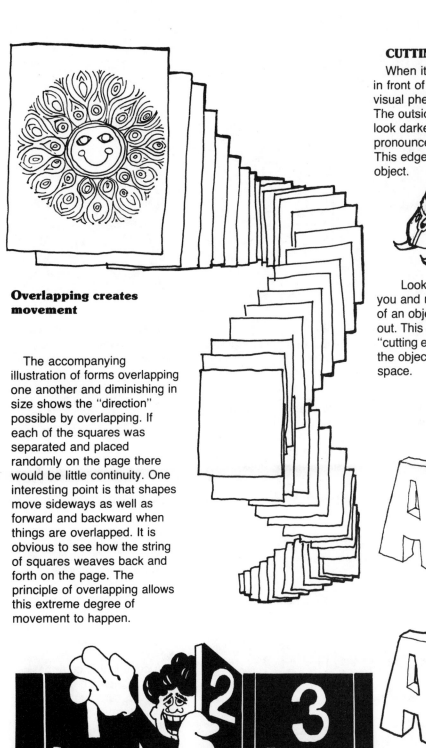

Overlapping creates movement

The accompanying illustration of forms overlapping one another and diminishing in size shows the "direction" possible by overlapping. If each of the squares was separated and placed randomly on the page there would be little continuity. One interesting point is that shapes move sideways as well as forward and backward when things are overlapped. It is obvious to see how the string of squares weaves back and forth on the page. The principle of overlapping allows this extreme degree of movement to happen.

CUTTING EDGE

When items are placed one in front of another a unique visual phenomenon occurs. The outside edge seems to look darker or more pronounced than the rest. This edge outlines the object.

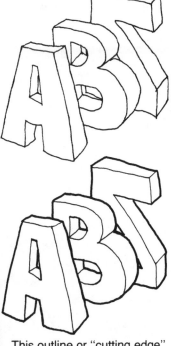

Look at the things around you and notice how the outline of an object seems to stand out. This outside edge we call a "cutting edge" because it "cuts" the object into its respective space.

This outline or "cutting edge" gives a more true sense of dimension and reality. Not all lines are drawn heavier, just the "cutting edge" such as has been accentuated in the bottom illustration of the letters of the alphabet.

Basic Shapes

A skill artists attempt to acquire as they begin to learn to draw is the ability to visualize complex objects as basic shapes. Artists usually rely on basic shapes to provide a skeleton for their drawings. From this skeleton they then evolve the drawing into a more finished form.

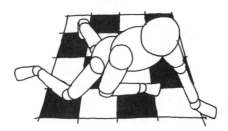

All objects that you see can be simplified into four basic shapes for drawing purposes. In other words, each of these shapes or a combination of them can be used to help you easily draw objects. The four basic drawing shapes are:

1. **Cylinder**

2. **Cube**

3. **Circle**

4. **Cone**

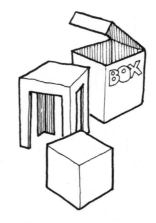

CUBE

You can draw **anything** by using these four basic forms as the basis for your drawn objects.

The examples above show how the basic form of a cube was utilized to help draw the objects. A cube forms the basis for a box, desk, chair, building, and a myriad of other things. When you simplify complex objects to basic shapes they are considerably easier to draw.

SPHERE

A sphere or cut portions of a sphere form most of the round items that we see. The ability to draw a truly spherical form is very useful in drawing.

CONE

A cone is the fourth basic shape. Ice cream cones, tents, many lids, are examples of conical forms. You will find it essential, but much less commonly used than the other three basic shapes.

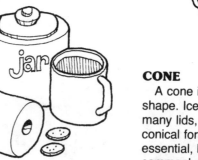

CYLINDER

The cylinder is the basis for many common objects. Cans, pots, jugs, pails, glasses are all made principally from the cylinder.

Everything you draw can be expressed as basic shapes.

18

Exercise: Get a magazine and draw the objects you find in some of its photos. Be sure to rely on the four basic forms to help you draw the "skeleton" of your object!

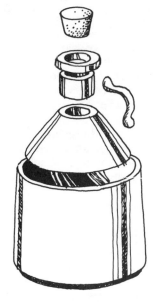

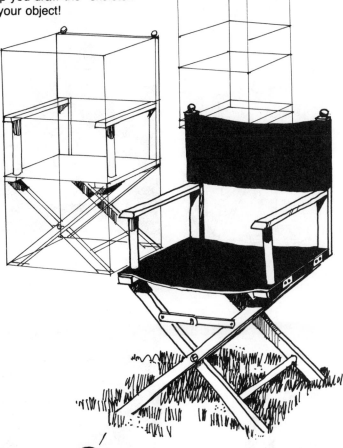

Form

Form is making a shape appear to have dimension and depth.

The items pictured here are typical examples of the combination of basic forms necessary to create a complex object. Most objects that occur in real life are a combination of the basic forms. These items are drawn with the help of the cone, cylinder, cube, and sphere. The understanding of how to draw the basic forms enables you to easily draw more complex objects.

The illustration on the right is a circle while the one on the left is a sphere. The shape is the same—a round circle—but one appears to have dimension and depth and the other appears to be flat.

Wrap-around lines and shading are drawing devices used to help give a three dimensional appearance to objects.

19

Basic Shapes

The essence of drawing is being able to visualize complex objects as basic shapes. The figures on these pages have been broken down into the basic shapes from which they can be easily drawn. The basic shapes are the same ones as discussed on page 18—the cube, sphere, cylinder, and cone.

When an artist learns to see a complex object as a combination of basic shapes, he then is well on his way to being able to draw accurately and well. It is quite simple to add detail once the form and proportion have been roughed in.

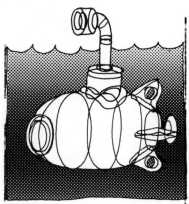

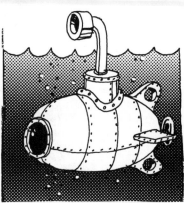

Most people don't realize that drawings usually evolve. Most people assume that a good artist can just sit down and draw a finished product. This isn't the case. All good artists have developed a method of roughing out a shape in basic and simple form as a beginning step. They then add, subtract, or change this rough drawing to arrive at a finished product. Their drawings evolve from a simple to a more complex and finished stage.

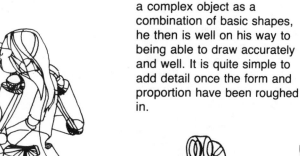

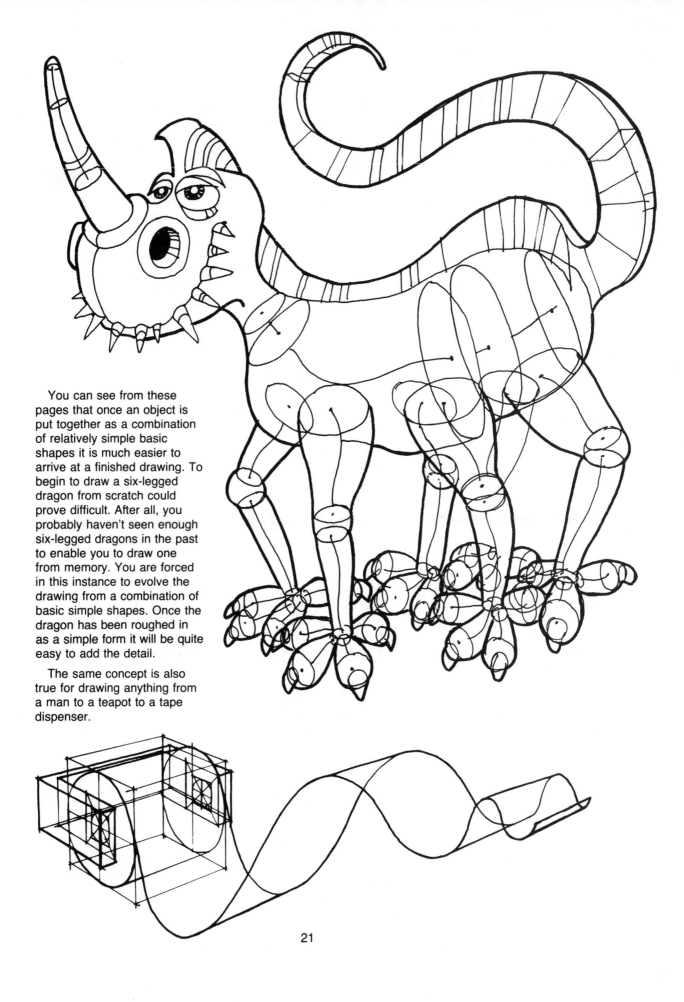

You can see from these pages that once an object is put together as a combination of relatively simple basic shapes it is much easier to arrive at a finished drawing. To begin to draw a six-legged dragon from scratch could prove difficult. After all, you probably haven't seen enough six-legged dragons in the past to enable you to draw one from memory. You are forced in this instance to evolve the drawing from a combination of basic simple shapes. Once the dragon has been roughed in as a simple form it will be quite easy to add the detail.

The same concept is also true for drawing anything from a man to a teapot to a tape dispenser.

21

Shadow

Stand a pencil on end and observe its shadow to determine the direction of the light source.

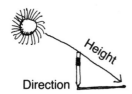

The height of the light source determines the length of the shadow.

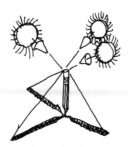

Shadow shows both the direction and the height of the light source.

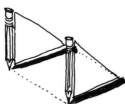

All objects form triangles with their shadows. Find the light source and determine the triangles formed to draw the cast shadows.

Solid objects (walls, surfaces, etc.) cast shadows in the same manner as a single pencil.

The height of the light source determines the angle of the triangle formed.

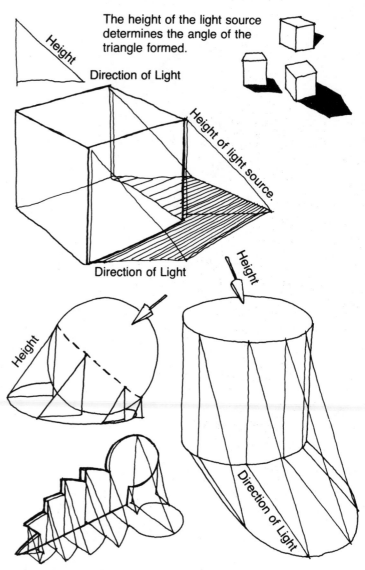

Emphasize the object, not its shadow.

Shadows can help greatly to show the form or detail of an object, but try not to let shadows become so dominant as to make it hard for the viewer to see the object.

A good tip to help you see what shadows are doing to your drawing or composition is to squint your eyes and notice just the dark areas. These dark areas are the most dominant part of the drawing and you can see what to do with them by squinting.

Shading

All objects have varying degrees of value or shaded portions. Subtle variations in lighting can create many degrees of shading on a single object. However, as you are learning it shouldn't be necessary to worry about more than 4 degrees of shading. You have surfaces which receive direct light and require no shading and surfaces which receive no light and are almost black. Between these two extremes you should have at least a light gray area and a dark gray area. These four variations should be sufficient to provide shading for most drawings. (On a rounded surface such as a cylinder these shades blend from white to black.)

Attention should be given to the fact that shadows are as much a part of the drawing as the form.

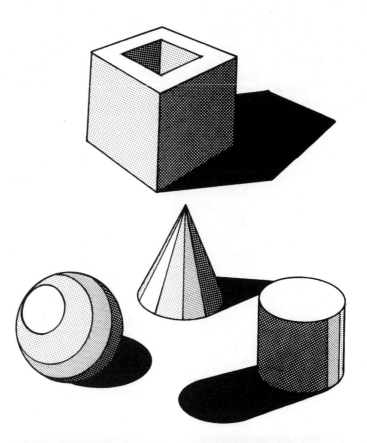

These drawings show 4 variations in shading. Obviously realistically shaded areas are not as defined as the areas of these drawings (white, light grey, dark grey, black). Truly shaded areas blend gradually.

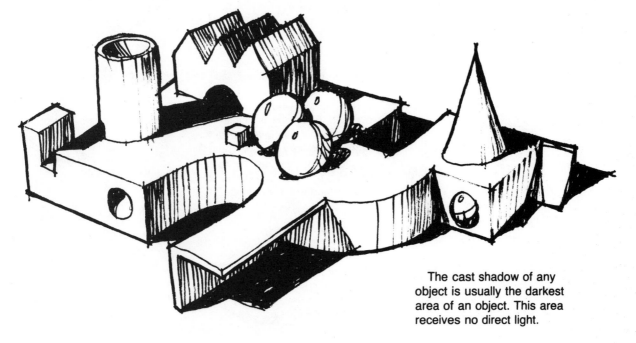

The cast shadow of any object is usually the darkest area of an object. This area receives no direct light.

Contour

Nature has a way of giving visual volume and shape to many things. The common caterpillar is an excellent example of the way nature gives visual shape to an object. The caterpillar is circled by natural lines which accentuate the appearance of its being cylindrical. The insect is rounded in shape, but the lines make it appear even more rounded.

We call these lines contour or wraparound lines.

The picture above is an example of common objects which have natural contour lines.

Look around; almost everything has contour or wraparound lines.

When you were looking for items with wraparound lines did you notice the natural lines on your fingers?

As you have observed, contour lines in nature help to give shape or volume. In drawing, the same principle can be applied to give an object imaginary shape. These wraparound lines can make two circles look like a donut as exemplified in the drawing.

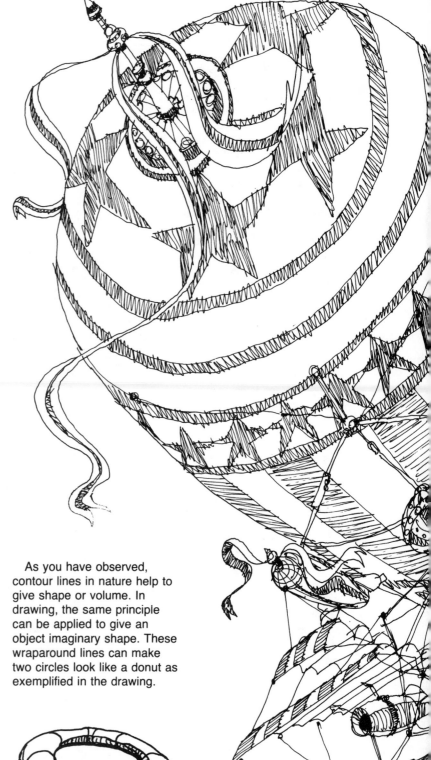

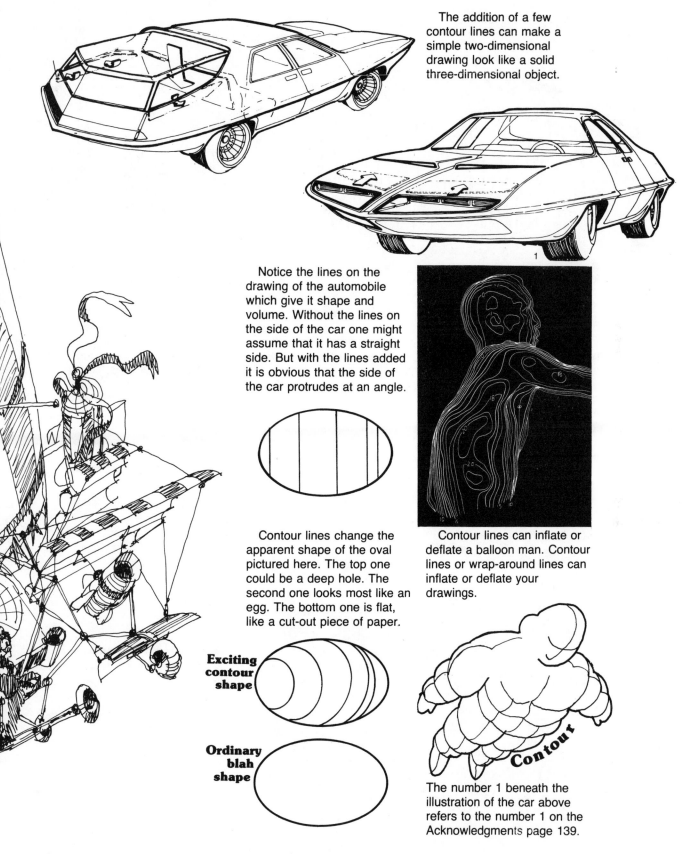

The addition of a few contour lines can make a simple two-dimensional drawing look like a solid three-dimensional object.

Notice the lines on the drawing of the automobile which give it shape and volume. Without the lines on the side of the car one might assume that it has a straight side. But with the lines added it is obvious that the side of the car protrudes at an angle.

Contour lines change the apparent shape of the oval pictured here. The top one could be a deep hole. The second one looks most like an egg. The bottom one is flat, like a cut-out piece of paper.

Exciting contour shape

Ordinary blah shape

Contour lines can inflate or deflate a balloon man. Contour lines or wrap-around lines can inflate or deflate your drawings.

Contour

The number 1 beneath the illustration of the car above refers to the number 1 on the Acknowledgments page 139.

25

Convergence

As you have looked at things in the distance you have noticed that they get smaller to the point where they finally vanish from sight. A string of telephone poles or a railroad track are excellent examples of diminishing size to a vanishing point. When items of equal size are placed in a line going away from you it is easy to see how they diminish in size and seem to vanish in the distance.

In order to create perspective in drawing a vanishing point is used. It works on the principle that parallel lines grow closer together and get gradually smaller until they vanish at a point on the horizon. If you are looking at something, then your eye determines where the vanishing point sits on the horizon. If you are drawing a picture then you as the artist determine where the vanishing point touches the horizon.

To help you visualize the relationship between vanishing points and horizon lines imagine yourself standing in water up to your eyes. You can see both above the water and below the water at the same time. At a point on the surface of the water and off in the distance, all things seem to disappear. This imaginary water surface is the horizon line and the point where all things disappear is the vanishing point.

If your eye is at water level then the things under water are seen from the top looking down and the things above water are seen from the bottom looking up.

The water level represents eye level—like standing in water up to your eyes.

The horizon line is always horizontal and level, never vertical or slanted.

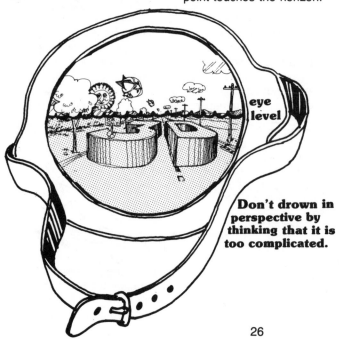

eye level

Don't drown in perspective by thinking that it is too complicated.

26

Try It!

Hold a clear piece of glass or stiff plexiglass stationary between you and an object. Now take a felt tip pen and trace what you see. If you are careful, and the glass is held completely stationary, you will end up with an excellent drawing in perfect perspective.

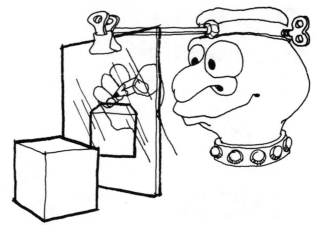

Hold a clear, hard surface in front of you and "Trace Nature." Be sure the surface is completely stationary.

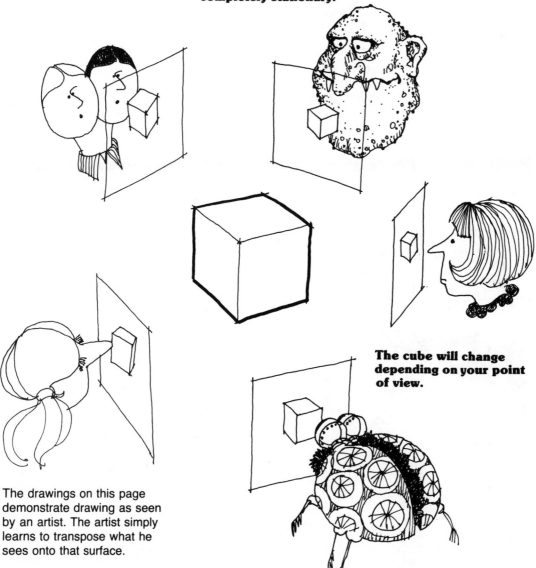

The cube will change depending on your point of view.

The drawings on this page demonstrate drawing as seen by an artist. The artist simply learns to transpose what he sees onto that surface.

One Point Perspective

One point perspective
3 kinds of lines
    vertical
    horizontal
    perspective

The boxes illustrated below are seen straight on so a single vanishing point is used to help draw them in perspective.

Notice how all the lines, except the vertical lines point toward a vanishing point. The vertical lines all remain parallel.

Also note that the farther away an object is from the vanishing point the more distortion occurs.

Drawing in perspective is a relatively easy task once you understand the principles. Because one point perspective is the simplest it is a good starting point.

When objects are directly looked upon, their form seems to diminish in size at the edges farthest from your vision. This diminishing size creates the illusion that the object would grow gradually smaller to a point where it would vanish at a point on the horizon.

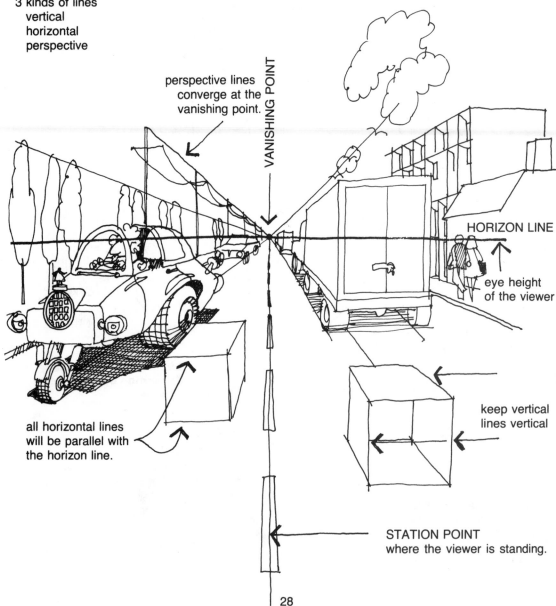

perspective lines converge at the vanishing point.

VANISHING POINT

HORIZON LINE

eye height of the viewer

all horizontal lines will be parallel with the horizon line.

keep vertical lines vertical

STATION POINT
where the viewer is standing.

Two Point Perspective

Two point perspective

2 kinds of lines
vertical
perspective

Objects that are seen from an angle seem to diminish in size in two directions. Notice how the boxes below are drawn with both sides of the box diminishing in size as the side gets farther away from you.

This is accomplished by having two vanishing points for drawing purposes located one at each side of the paper. Both points are located on the same horizon line. The farther apart the two vanishing points are, the less the degree of convergence of the sides of the boxes.

All vertical lines remain parallel just as in one point perspective.

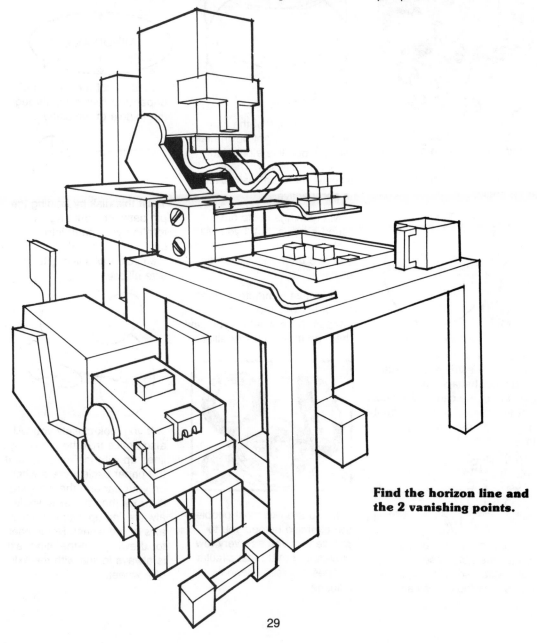

Find the horizon line and the 2 vanishing points.

29

Ellipse
Circles in Perspective

Ellipse, huh? Well, it might sound new but it's a common element in our lives. An ellipse is simply a circle seen at an angle.

As you look straight down on top of a can you see a circle. This same circle takes on different shapes as the position of the can is changed. Set the can up straight in front of you with the top at eye level.

From this angle you no longer are able to see a circle but instead see a straight line across the top of the can.

As you lower the can you see more of a circle, but the top does not look exactly round until your eyes are directly over the top of the can looking straight down.

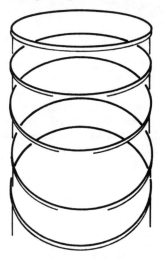

The positions of the can other than straight down make the top look like elongated circles or ellipses. These ellipses then are really circles in perspective.

Many things in life have round shapes, but if you will look closely you will notice that you see them most often as ellipses.

Take just a minute and list ten items which have circle shapes. Note whether you saw them as true circles or ellipses.

If you are like most people the exercise helped you to realize that you see very few circles, but that most circular shapes are really seen as ellipses.

By understanding the anatomy of an ellipse you will be better able to draw one. An ellipse has a major and a minor axis. The major axis is an imaginary line which connects the two widest points of the ellipse.

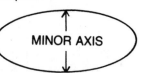

The minor axis connects the two closest points of the ellipse.

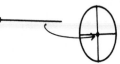

Find or cut a circle out of paper and stick a pin through the middle of the circle.

Twist this disk by holding the pin between your fingers and rotating your hand into different angles. You will notice the circle looks like different size ellipses.

If you look closely you will also notice that the pin always lines up with the minor axis. If the paper circle were a wheel on your car and the pin were the axle then the axle would always line up with the minor axis of the wheel. Remember for drawing that the minor axis is always in line with the axle of a wheel.

Drawing a circle in perspective is very, very simple. It's just like copying. First draw an ordinary square with a circle in it. Connect the corners where the circle touches the square.

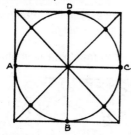

Note where the circle touches the square (A B C D) and the proportions of the diagonal lines to the circle. The circle crosses these diagonals two-thirds the distance from the center.

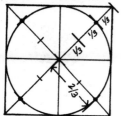

First draw a square in perspective. Divide the square into 4 equal quarters by drawing lines connecting the center of the sides of the square.

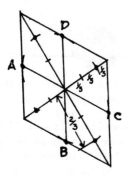

Measure ⅔ out on the diagonal from the center to find the line of your circle.

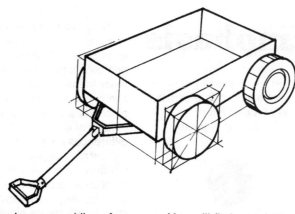

Now draw curved lines from the points of the center of the sides of the square. When these are all connected you will have drawn a circle in perspective.

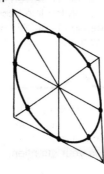

Now draw lines from the corners of the square making an X in the center of the squares. Where these lines cross is the center of your circle in perspective. You will notice, however, that the center of the square is not where the major and minor axes cross. The center of the circle always falls upon the line which forms the minor axis, but it does not fal on the point where the major and minor axes cross.

You will find many, many occasions in drawing where a circle drawn in perspective will be needed.

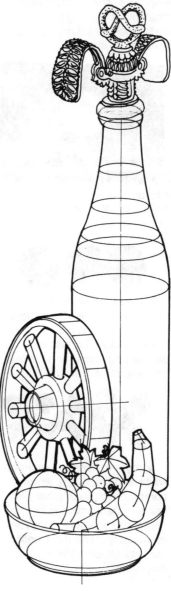

Emphasis

Emphasis is used in drawing to attract attention to a certain portion of a drawing or to dramatize certain aspects.

One black dot in a white field is an example of emphasis. The contrast of the small black area against the white background draws attention to the dot.

A white dot against a black background also creates emphasis. Attention is drawn to the white dot.

The more dots the less emphasis there is. Three dots can still emphasize a point, but the more dots the less the degree of contrast and the less effective the emphasis.

Many dots form a pattern of white and black dots which compete with each other and neither one dominates or demands more attention. The more competition for attention the less effective the emphasis.

Many different components in a drawing can cause emphasis. Light against dark and color against no color, are other forms of contrast. Detail can cause emphasis when placed in a picture dominated by lack of detail. Size differences create emphasis in a drawing. Any pattern break will draw attention and thereby emphasize a portion of a drawing. Any unexpected change will create emphasis.

The line below is an excellent example of how emphasis works. Notice that the straight line holds no intrigue at all. However, when a variation in the line occurs your attention is quickly drawn to that variation.

One jog in the line is emphasis. The unexpected variation in the straight line demands your attention.

Two jogs in the line aren't quite as interesting.

The more jogs in the line the less emphasis. When you have a number of jogs in the line as shown here a straight portion would cause emphasis.

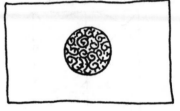

The stronger the contrast the better the emphasis. If you want portions of a black and white drawing to stand out, then place them next to the most extreme contrast possible . . . black next to white, for example. Do the same with color . . . bright vivid colors against dark drab colors.

Emphasis in a drawing often takes precedent over reality. A portion of a drawing will probably not be white against a black background in real life, but you may wish to make it appear that way for the sake of emphasis which is necessary in your composition for good design.

You manipulate emphasis!

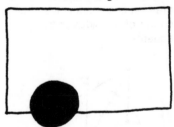

This illustrates white against detail.

Just the opposite is detail against white.

A dot intersecting a line or a dot out of the margin illustrates

the impact (or emphasis) when something happens out of context. Emphasis is determined by the inter-relationship (or lack of relationship) of things.

Context is the key to emphasis!

The degree of emphasis caused by any variation in a drawing depends on the content in which it is used within that drawing. For example, a large black dot on a white background will not emphasize any one portion of that drawing. The black dot needs to be small to draw attention to it.

Distort for emphasis.

The drawing of the barn contains many areas where the principle of emphasis is used to demand attention. The white against the dark creates a direction for the eye to follow as it emphasizes certain portions of the drawing. It is this manipulation of light against dark which is most often used to compose a picture. The artist creates illusions by the contrasts and makes the picture hold together by causing your eye to follow a certain direction.

DESIGN

OPT

You are a designer! You design every day of your life. During each day you decide whether to make the most of that day or just to let it pass by. If you don't willfully consider each day or the things you do, then you become a designer by neglect.

Design is the optimum use of different tools around you to the creation of a better solution to life and the problems which confront you. Design is finding the optimum in a particular set of circumstances. It is finding the best solution within a given set of parameters.

Design is for people. Design is a responsibility of everyone. Most animals do not have the same capability to govern their surroundings as does man. This ability to govern and control our surroundings also carries the responsibility to do just that—design our lives and the things around us in the best possible way.

Design is the interface in the relationship between man and his environment. It is the optimum combination of man with his environment. It is man living in, cooperating with, using correctly and beautifully those things of nature which surround everyone and

make this world the place that it is. Design is respect for aesthetics, technology, life, and efficiency all wrapped in one.

Some examples of man in his surroundings may tend to demonstrate how design actually must claim the responsibility for the environment of man.

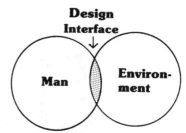

Think of yourself in a modern airport. You will remember the long rows of chairs connected one to another in a long monotonous line. There is no way for three or more people to sit side by side and converse. Since the chairs are arranged in a row only two can converse because the third finds himself uncomfortably in the middle or left out of a conversation. If there is to be conversation, it can only occur between people standing in clusters. These places are hardest on families with young children and gregarious people who like to talk to each other. For children, the long

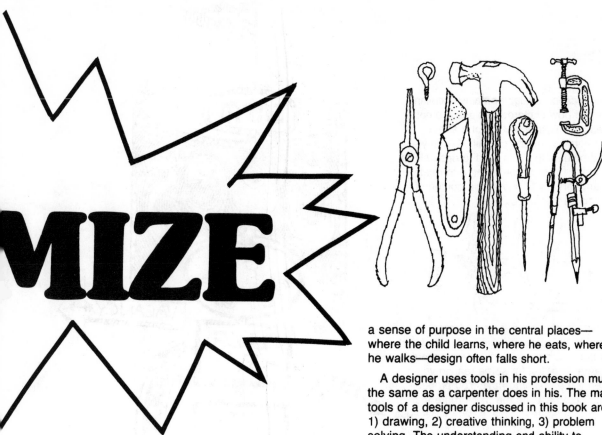

MIZE

parallel rows of chairs resemble a race course and they run it to everyone's displeasure. A grandmother may hear her grandson talking five seats down the row, but she cannot begin to understand what he is saying. Her sense of separation begins as soon as the family sits down in the institutional row of chairs. To vary colors and mount posters on the wall makes the area prettier to look at. But that is no compensation for a design that deliberately interferes with human relations.

Look about you in the schools. The building usually is well laid out. The surroundings are well gardened. The facades look clean, though they're often hard to distinguish from those of factories. Whether such design makes children feel comfortable, happy and secure within the building and whether it induces children to like learning, seems to fall low in the order of architectural consideration.

Often our schools have good auditoriums, libraries, gymnasiums and swimming pools. Sometimes they have impressive entrance halls, but this is usually the limit of good design. When it comes to comfort, beauty, and a sense of purpose in the central places—where the child learns, where he eats, where he walks—design often falls short.

A designer uses tools in his profession much the same as a carpenter does in his. The major tools of a designer discussed in this book are 1) drawing, 2) creative thinking, 3) problem solving. The understanding and ability to correctly use these design tools is as important to the success of a designer as knowing how to use a saw, hammer and screwdriver is to the success of the carpenter.

Other sections of the book discuss drawing, problem solving and creative thinking as tools of design. This section shows you how to apply those tools to specific design situations.

A very effective design process is called the **SAFE** design. **SAFE** stands for **S**imple, **A**ppropriate, **F**unctional and **E**conomical. If you can employ **SAFE** DESIGN in the context of Creative Problem Solving, you'll be well on your way to placing Man comfortably in his environment—which is what Good Design is all about.

SAFE DESIGN is the key to this section. **SIMPLE**, **APPROPRIATE**, **FUNCTIONAL** and **ECONOMICAL** Designs.

SAFE

Communication design contains excellent examples of how cluttered designs are not good designs. Take a picture of a street. Almost all typical streets contain so many unrelated objects that it is hard to understand what is going on. It becomes hard to relate closely and directly to any single portion of information on that street.

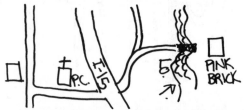

Have you ever looked for an address and been unable to locate the building? Often that very address was marked in large numbers or with a huge sign, but for some reason you didn't see it the first time past. You probably ended up going around the block more than once trying to locate the place. Why? Because you are only able to easily absorb ONE piece of information at a time. Your mind is able to absorb about five related or peripheral pieces of information at one time but only ONE piece thoroughly and easily.

Take the examples of the faces/vase below. When you look at this what do you see? You have undoubtedly seen this puzzle before and can therefore pick out both the vase and the faces. The fact that you know there are two pieces of completely different information is no consolation, because your mind still tries to isolate one piece of information at a time. You have to almost force yourself to see both the vase and the faces at the same time. You probably didn't realize that you were so narrow-minded. Get used to it, because you'll be that way all your life when it comes to the amount of information your mind will easily assimilate at one time.

What do you see? One thing at a time, right? Either a vase or faces.

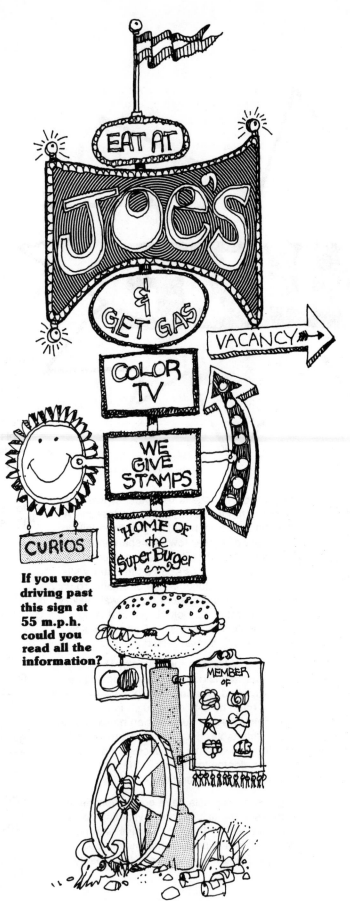

If you were driving past this sign at 55 m.p.h. could you read all the information?

Have you ever seen a sign like the one on the previous page? What does it say? How much do you think you could get out of that sign as you travel down the road at 55 miles per hour and talk to a friend in the next seat? Count the different pieces of information on the sign on the opposite page. If you found 20, that is about right.

Now compare the sign above. Close your eyes and think of yourself traveling along a busy highway at 55 miles per hour passing signs all along the way. Just how much would you have gotten out of the complicated confusing sign as compared to this simplified one? The clean, simple, direct approach of the one sign communicates much more effectively than the complex one. If you get enough information to help you decide whether to return to the restaurant, you have understood all that the owner wants. The simple sign better communicates a clean comfortable place to eat good food than does the complex sign. Think about it!

Do you remember the old tire swing? Perhaps your grandparents had one, or maybe you were lucky enough to have one of your own. Those were the days. Modern advertising and trends here all but eliminated the old tire swing. Instead, we now have poorly built, dangerous and not nearly as fun to ride in new metal swings. It would seem much wiser to use some of those old worn tires and make a swing rather than settle for the new unsafe version. The new one will wear out sooner (have you ever heard of an old tire swing that has worn out because of use—it would take many miles of use to wear out that sturdy tire). The new one will pinch you, but have you ever heard of anyone being pinched by an old tire? The tire will swing higher. It will not gash your head if it happens to swing into you. Sometimes we give up much in exchange for things that really are of inferior quality and poor design. Because it's new doesn't mean it's better.

Say and do only what is necessary.

Say your piece then shut up.
Simplify, summarize and stop. The best design is the one that is simple and works well with the least amount of trouble.

SAFE

In our modern society and technology much of what is done is OVERDONE. The drawing of the chair below typifies this point. Chairs now available (in deluxe model of course) will recline, rock, massage, or just jiggle you a bit. These chairs are available in fake leather grain, fake wood grain or fake chrome. They are available with built-in radios, built-in stereos and even built-in televisions. Some of them are complex, expensive and impractical. To say the least many chairs are overdone.

The more complicated an item is, the more that can go wrong. More problems make the item more expensive and not very practical.

Look at the director's chair below. It has been around for a long time. It is inexpensive, comfortable and well designed. It can be stored easily, repaired easily and replaced at little cost when it is worn out. A director's chair will not serve all purposes, but it is a well designed and useful chair in the right setting.

The paper clip is an example of excellent simple design. It holds papers together well, is easily attached and removed, inexpensive, and easy to manufacture. There are other fasteners that hold papers together better under specific conditions. Staples, for example, are great for holding papers together permanently. But nothing works better to hold papers temporarily together than does a paper clip.

The band-aid is another example of excellent, but simple design. Nothing works much better than the band-aid for small abrasions. It doesn't work well for deep lacerations, but it wasn't designed for that use. For what it was intended to do, it is an adequate, simple solution to a problem.

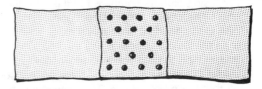

The items shown below are examples of simple design. They are from the Braun design collection which is noted for its very well designed and simplified appliances. All items are honest, easily operated, easily maintained and serviced, and visually appealing in design.

4

The zipper is an example of excellent, simple design. It has been around for a long time and will probably remain for a few more years to come. It is a tight, simple fastener which can be easily applied to a great number of uses.

Simplicity in design depends upon the context in which it is used. For example, a tin can and string form an adequate "telephone" for children to use over the backyard fence. It doesn't cost much and is easily constructed and maintained. A more complex telephone is required, however, if we wish to make long distant and easily heard calls.

Simplicity in design depends upon the technology available at the time it was created. We are fortunate to have stereo and extremely high quality sound reproduction equipment. However, the early phonograph models were just as well designed and creative—if you take into consideration the technology available at the time they existed. The important thing is to fully take advantage of current technology in creating a workable simple design or invention.

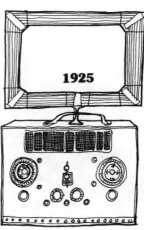

1925

1970

A 1925 radio weighed 57 lbs.

A 1970 radio weighs a few ounces.

Simple
SAFE

This page contains examples of simple, effective designs or inventions.

The old Kodak Brownie camera was a well designed camera. It was simple, did the job and was easy to use. It sold well.

The polaroid is another example of a well-designed camera. The advent of new, almost instantaneous developing film allowed camera inventors new latitudes in camera design. The polaroid is an amazing breakthrough.

Then came the instamatic camera. Technology allowed the addition of the automatic eye, better film and therefore a smaller case, and actually an easier camera to operate. It's a very good example of excellent, simple design.

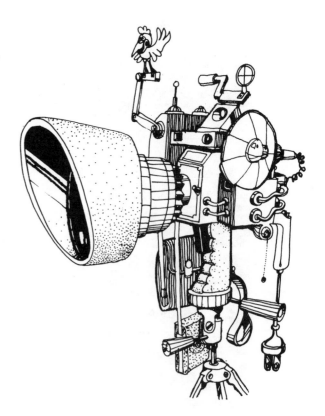

5

Logos are types of communication design. The symbols adopted by companies to communicate their name often demonstrate excellent design.

Note the simplicity and easily remembered design for the Bell logo.

And have you ever seen this symbol before?

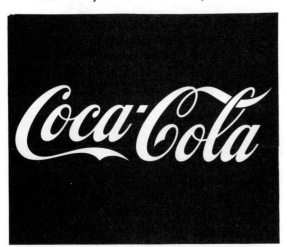

Logos which incorporate words or names into their design are often more easily remembered than just graphic design logos. Heavy advertising has made the Coca Cola name familiar to us all. The unique design of the words has made the name and symbol easy to remember.

Mary Had a Little Lamb

Mary was the legal owner of a diminutive, potential sheep, whose haliberments were as innocent of coloring as congealed atmospheric vapor. And no matter where the ultimate destination of Mary's peregrinations, after infantile southward was positively certain to caper.

It shadowed little Mary to the local dispensary of knowledge one diurnal division ofttime, which was contrary to all written and unwritten precedents. At the sight of the miniature mutton gamboling gaily at the front of learning, there was a considerable mirth and aportivens in the ranks of the seminary attendants.

Compare this version of "Mary Had A Little Lamb" with the original poem.

Is the design honest or is it trying to be something it is not?

SAFE

SAFE design states that whatever the occasion, use, or design function the form should be of an appropriate nature.

Goethe wrote a very scholarly sounding essay dealing with appropriate form: "I cannot approve of furnishing entire rooms in an imitated style and of living in the surroundings of a bygone period. It is always a kind of masquerade which, in the long run, does not bode well, but will rather have a detrimental influence on the people who indulge in it. For it stands in contradiction to the living days into which we are born and emanates from an empty and hollow attitude and mentality which is thus confirmed. Upon a gay winter's evening one might well attend a masquerade dressed as a Turk, but what, alas, would we think of a person who would show himself in such disguise all year round? We would assume either that he is crazy or, at all events, disposed to become so."

Look at the final solution setting and how your design will fit into it.

Doesn't it seem a little strange to see the snowy white vapor trails of a huge modern jet plane show in the background of a cowboy and Indian movie which supposedly took place sometime in the 1800's? Have you ever seen this or similar modern attractions appear in movies depicting another era?

It would seem strange indeed to see the Father of our Country—George Washington—commanding his troops from the cockpit of a new Mack Truck.

Not only should design coordinate items as to their correct time in history, but design should also coordinate their function, setting and use in modern time. For example, a table should appear to be and do what it is designed for. If it is to be a table to eat on, then it should not resemble an operating table, a carpenter's table or a gambling table. The table should be comfortable and inviting as a place to eat. Good design tastefully coordinates beauty, style, time and function of the many elements which constitute any specific design situation.

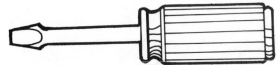

You could get fouled up if your design solution doesn't fit its final working setting!

Good design means coordinating today's skills and knowledge to arrive at a working finished product. It would be futile to design large, expensive, gas guzzling automobiles under today's energy conditions. A fuel conserving machine would be much better accepted and certainly more appropriate.

Machines that are built to be compatible with other existing, similar machinery, are much more appropriate than "odd-ball" inventions. It would be pointless to design a machine that could not be fixed by using standard tools such as wrenches and screwdrivers. Appropriate design means that creation is compatible with today's knowledge, technology, tools, and machinery.

There once was a handsome young fellow
Whose favorite color was yellow.
He gave his wife Anna
A phone like a banana
With a ring that was soft, sweet, and mellow.

Anna loved her new telephone.
She shined it each day 'til it shone.
But when company came
She would have to explain
Because each one tried to eat it all gone.

One day when she was away
The phone rang and it rang all the day
An impatient friend
Thought the ringing she'd end
And went in, but to her dismay—

A telephone she could not find
Though she looked in and out and behind
With her appetite grown
She gobbled the phone
That's the end of the phone and our rhyme.

Corinne Reed

Hello Hello

SAFE

Another word for appropriate design might be "Honesty." Is the design honest in what it communicates, or does?

Is the Venus de Milo an appropriate design? Do the clock in the stomach and the statue honestly relate? Do they fit together well in time and place (electric clocks were undoubtedly a little known luxury afforded the Roman nobility)? Are the feelings and message this statue convey honest and appropriate?

**Tick Tock
Tick Tock
Tick Tock**

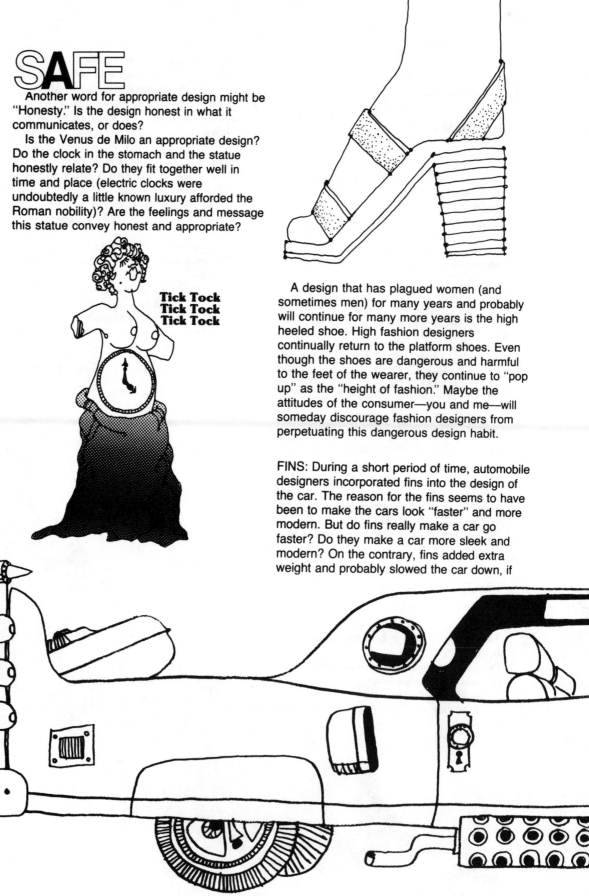

A design that has plagued women (and sometimes men) for many years and probably will continue for many more years is the high heeled shoe. High fashion designers continually return to the platform shoes. Even though the shoes are dangerous and harmful to the feet of the wearer, they continue to "pop up" as the "height of fashion." Maybe the attitudes of the consumer—you and me—will someday discourage fashion designers from perpetuating this dangerous design habit.

FINS: During a short period of time, automobile designers incorporated fins into the design of the car. The reason for the fins seems to have been to make the cars look "faster" and more modern. But do fins really make a car go faster? Do they make a car more sleek and modern? On the contrary, fins added extra weight and probably slowed the car down, if

46

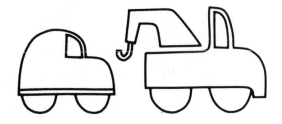

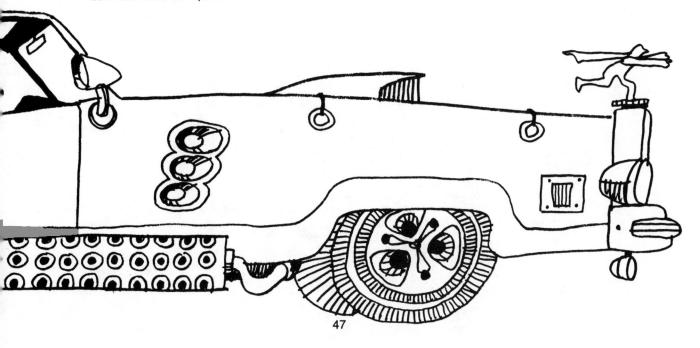

anything. And instead of making the car seem more modern, the fins dated the car so explicitly that the design showed "age" in the very year that it was conceived. Instead of allowing the design of the car to remain contemporary and last for considerable time, the fins outdated a car very rapidly.

MUFFLERS: What is the reason so many people put large mufflers along the outside of their automobile? Do these mufflers cut down noise or work more efficiently than regular size mufflers? Probably not, in fact many of the large mufflers along the sides of cars aren't functional anyway, just ornamental.

HOLES IN THE SIDE: No doubt the holes in the side are for ornament and serve no real function.

HOOD SCOOP: If the hood scoop functioned it might allow the engine to run more efficiently, but most hood scoops are for ornament.

BUT WOULDN'T THIS BE A NEAT CAR TO HAVE! The responsibility of good design lies not only with the designer, but also with the many other people who tolerate or even accept poor design. Consumers perpetuate poor design by buying and using items that are inappropriately designed. Sometimes no choice exists, but most often it is simply that the consumer disregards good design and buys because of emotion rather than intellect. Being better informed consumers and buying for a reason, rather than buying because of advertising or because it's the "in thing," will result in better products.

SAFE [3]

SAFE

We have talked about function in SAFE design being the fact that good design works as it is planned to. But the function is actually more than just the fact that "it works."

SMITH-CORONA AMERICAN SIMPLIFIED KEYBOARD

CT — CHANGEABLE TYPE   RK — REPEAT KEY   © SCM CORPORATION 1973

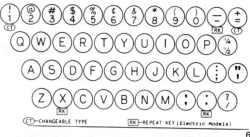

STANDARD KEYBOARD

CT — CHANGEABLE TYPE   RK — REPEAT KEY (Electric Models)

6

**Do you think
they'll know you're behind me?**

Humans are the designers with the ability to easily manipulate the function of items. It is necessary that function considers use, context, surroundings, by-products and waste, incroachment on others, etc. Designers become the stewards of their creations and are responsible for the benefits and problems produced as a result of their work.

The first typewriter keyboard was designed as a stumbling block for the typist. Original typewriters could not function mechanically as fast as a person could type and so a confusing keyboard was designed to slow down the typist. This same keyboard has survived to modern times unchanged. Research, however, has developed a new keyboard which is designed for the speed our new machines are capable of. It will be interesting to see how long before use of the keyboard can be updated now that habits have so strongly established the old style keyboard as part of our lives.

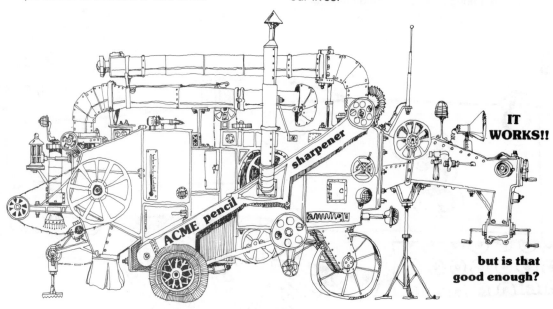

ACME pencil sharpener

IT WORKS!!

but is that good enough?

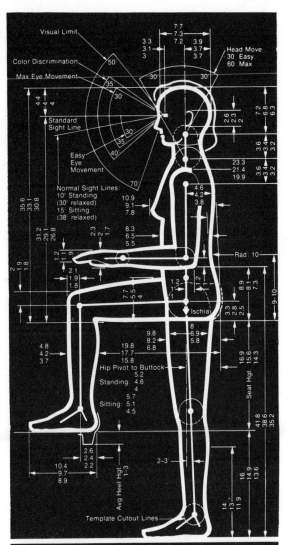

Make sure the item will work well. For centuries items have been designed and built for use by humans. In recent years engineers recognized the value of knowing the parameters of function of the human body. This relatively new additional and precise knowledge enables manufacturing of products that can be better used by man and safer to him.

Don't stand around—DESIGN!

Does it look like what it does?

Research by a clothes iron manufacturing company showed that 4 holes in a steam iron worked just as well as the conventional 9-hole steam iron. The consumer however, wouldn't believe that 4 holes worked just as well so the iron didn't sell. The iron manufacturer had to discontinue the line or drill 5 dummy holes which fooled the consumer into thinking he was getting a 9-hole and supposedly a better iron.

The extra holes in the iron didn't make one bit of difference in the performance of the iron, but they became an essential part of the design of that iron when the total picture was included. Without the extra 5 holes the consumer wouldn't buy the product, so it was a design failure though it functioned perfectly.

Let's take some other examples. A brochure set in five point type could contain all the information it was supposed to, but if intended for the elderly it probably wouldn't work. Most elderly can't see small type. Realizing just this fact, Reader's Digest has a special edition which is published regularly now. This one edition of the Digest is set in large type and is intended for the elderly to read.

Do you find it difficult to read this? I find it very difficult to see. If you continue reading this your eyes will start to burn and you may begin to see double, triple or worse. If you insist on reading this, please find a magnifying glass or the end of a soda pop bottle—the magnification may help.

Fire extinguishers have been designed which are very attractive. They blend well with their surroundings. Visually they are very well designed, but what they boast in visual appearance they lack in the ability to function. Some of these fire extinguishers are so well camouflaged that when fire strikes, the would-be user cannot figure out how to retrieve the extinguisher from its attractive case. The fire burns on and the extinguisher sits looking pretty until it is charred beyond recognition.

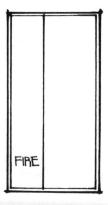

A reportedly true story is often repeated among designers about a household fire extinguisher. You are familiar with the kitchen demonstration areas of some large department and furniture stores. It seems that a home economist was employed by one store to give cooking demonstrations to customers. During one demonstration, as luck would have it, some grease caught fire and rapidly spread across the store to hanging curtains. The frantic cook sent customers and sales clerks scurrying to find a fire extinguisher to put out the blaze. A familiar red industrial extinguisher was located and used to douse the fire, but it was too late to do much good. Curtains, stove, cabinets, and a good portion of the kitchen were all charred or damaged by fire, heat and smoke. And among the ashes stood a cabinet with the letters 'FIRE' written across it. You guessed it . . . a fire extinguisher was burned with everything else.

Design can go too far. The fire extinguisher was designed to fit well with the decor of the kitchen. The only problem was that since it was not a familiar design, and because it was not easily recognized, it became useless. A fire is a panic situation, and with all else, design must take into consideration the circumstances surrounding the use of designed appliances and the people who will use those appliances.

Does the chair pictured below seem comfortable to you? It didn't sell very well because it looked unstable. People were afraid to sit in it because it appeared as though it would fall over or break. It would neither break nor fall over, but since it looked as though it would we must conclude that it was not designed well from a functional point of view.

New technology has produced some extremely strong alloys which would allow us to design tables with legs almost as thin as wires. But how do you think these tables would sell or look in the context they will be used? Would you have confidence placing a good set of china on a table with wires for legs? Things that work well should look like they would work well.

It will hold you, but does it look like it will?

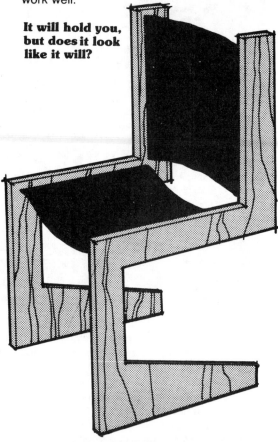

Many aspects affect the functional design in SAFE design besides just the fact that it "works." An item must be designed to work in a given situation or the context in which it is to be used. It must not be considered only from an engineering point of view, but also from a social, financial, mental, physical, human engineering and many other points of view. It must work in the context for which it is planned.

Have you ever walked into a glass door? Have you ever been in an office of glass where you felt like the whole world was looking at you? Have you ever been in a building built primarily of glass that became unbearably hot when the sun shone upon it? Modern architecture has developed some "beautiful" buildings that don't function very well. If people are to live in a building then it should function with people in mind. Glass can form good doors but it needs to be marked so that people don't walk through thinking that it is an open passage way. Glass can form protective walls, but it sometimes does not afford privacy where it might be needed. (The mental picture of a patient in a dental chair in a glass building always comes to mind. An architect in my home town designed a new medical complex with walls of glass. Every time I walk by that building I suffer with or am embarrassed by some patient who loses his composure as the pain contorts his body.)

Some of the new buildings are beautiful as they reflect their surroundings in the walls of glass. It is unfortunate, however, that the inhabitants must pay thousands for draperies, air conditioning, and heating so that they can be comfortable and have some degree of privacy.

SAFE

Economics deals with more than just the cost. It deals with cost to purchase, life, serviceability, ease of production, availability of supplies, need to the buyer, visual acceptability, cultural acceptability, aesthetic appeal, etc.

$400.

The demand/cost ratio of a product must be carefully considered. How many ball point pens would you buy if they cost $400 each? That is approximately what the first pens cost to produce. Fortunately mass production has lowered the figure to just a few cents per pen. New products, designs, or inventions may be costly initially, but if the idea seems profitable in the long run, the risk might well be worth it.

Designers have the responsibility to provide[8] consumers with the best economic choices available. Products are purchased to meet the needs of status, efficiency, economy, operation, maintenance and so forth. Not all items sell because they are the best buy. The designer, however, has the responsibility to give the consumer the best choices available to meet his specific needs.

Chairs are bought according to use, price, and need. The office furniture shown above is expensive, well built and very good furniture. It meets the needs of its use in the office. The bean bag chair below would not serve well in most offices, but is better for home use and costs much less. Price is not necessarily the determining factor of the quality of an item; it merely is a part of the overall economic value along with need, type of use, durability, etc.

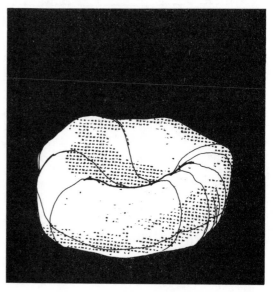

MORE with LESS

"One man's trash is another man's treasure."

We live in a world where the conservation and wise use of what we have is important. Indications are that conservation will become an increasing consideration in the future. The designer will have greater responsibility to develop better products which have long life, can be reused, or utilize waste materials of other products in beneficial ways.

Let's look at some examples of "MORE FOR LESS."

BLIMP—a blimp or dirigible provides better ton per mile cost ratio than current transportation. (If speed or safety is the most important consideration then jets or trains might be better).

DOORMATS—Used automobile fan belts can be converted into sturdy doormats.

MILORGANITE—A lawn fertilizer produced from cleaned and processed human waste.

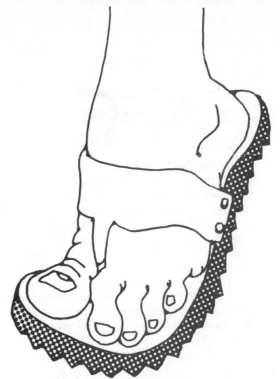

HUARACHES—Sandal type shoes made in Mexico use discarded tires for the soles.

SAFE DESIGN-ECONOMICS

The SAFE design method which has been discussed on previous pages depends upon the cooperative mingling of four principles of design. A design must be SIMPLE, be APPROPRIATE in the context it is used, FUNCTION correctly and be ECONOMICALLY sound. Designs which lack one of these traits will most often fail or at least be poor designs.

Economics in good design is the ability to get the most with the least, to get maximum results with minimum cost and work, and to get the optimum results in a given set of circumstances.

MORE WITH LESS has a point of no return. Don't economize or conserve to the extent that the final produce is of no real value. A stool, for example, needs at least three legs to stand alone.

SAFE

DESIGN ECONOMICS

ECONOMICS in design holds more weight than one might presume. The creation of a design, innovative idea or new invention waits for the economics of the siutation before a final step. If the money, materials, time or demand for the product are not there, then all else is to no avail. No matter how good the idea, without the necessary resources, the idea might as well be non-existent. Along with all else, a good design must fit within the framework of being economically sound.

Evaluate your design with SAFE so it won't go down the drain.

The geodesic dome is another example of [9] economic consideration. The relative newness of the structural technique produces some limitations, but structural strength, design, lower cost and many other factors may make the dome more popular as acceptable architecture in the future. It is known to be an excellent building technique; it is just that other factors must complement the structure. Heating, lighting, space division, etc. all present new and interesting challenges for the builder of the geodesic dome. Stacking cardboard boxes in a geodesic dome warehouse, for example, would cause much space to be wasted because the walls curve while the boxes are rectangular.

MANY FACTORS INFLUENCE DESIGN ECONOMICS

Economics in design is evident in many things. High impact plastics exemplify the intrusion of economics into luggage, appliances and home tools. The plastics enable manufacturers to build a more durable, safer, cleaner and less expensive product.

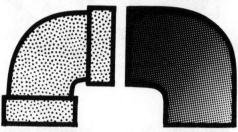

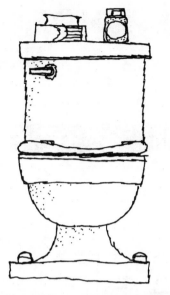

METAL PIPE	**PLASTIC PIPE**
Needs thread—Requires special tools for threading and tightening connections	No Thread—Connected by glue
	Easy to Cut—
Difficult to cut—Time consuming process to obtain special lengths of pipe	Flexible—Can be easily bent into long flowing curves to bypass stationary obstacles
Not Flexible—Rigid metal	Not extremely durable—Original plastic pipe wasn't heat resistant, it broke more easily than metal and was often chewed through by rats.
Very durable—Heat resistant, cold resistant, not bothered by rodents	
Requires special tools and knowledge to use. Professionals rather than handymen are primary users	Easy to use—Can be assembled by most handymen with little difficulty
Meets building code requirements. Old product, tested and reliable	Doesn't meet all building codes—it is a relatively new product and building codes will need to change as the product improves in order to insure more extensive use

An often overlooked factor in the economy of design is safety. Safer things are, in the long run, less expensive and more profitably used. Safety is directly related to economy.

GET AHEAD OF THE PROBLEM

Economy in design demands that long lasting solutions be achieved rather than stop-gap measures. Efficient, clean use of our nation's water supply has been spotlighted by environmental awareness. Many individuals have responded by placing bricks in their toilets to conserve the amount of water they use. In the end, however, the real solution will eventually be the designing of a more efficient toilet to help everyone better use their limited water supplies and maintain clean rivers and streams. Bricks don't work effectively because toilets weren't designed that way.

Good Design is a balance.

Good design must balance many factors in order to produce effective results. Needs and demands must be weighed against the factors of production, emotion, morals, availability of materials, cost, use, etc. A design cannot stand alone. It will be acted upon by these factors of "economy." In the end the design will either be produced, bought and used or discarded as just another good idea that couldn't make it.

SAFE

What is good design? How can you tell a good designer from a poor one?

Design depends upon its context. Many people feel that good design is merely something that 'looks good.' But is this enough? What about a brochure that looks good, but doesn't communicate? What about a book that looks good but doesn't sell? Good design 'depends.'

This book can't be called 'fine art.' It is not formal, it is not refined, and it is not pretty; but hopefully it communicates and teaches in a visually pleasing and enjoyable way. If it reaches the reader, is visually pleasing, and is fun to learn from then we contend that it is designed well.

Complaints about designers often go like this:

Ad Agency about the architect . . .
Sure, the building 'looks good' but it can't be built. . .or. . .Sure, the building 'looks good' but it will cost another $10,000,000 to have those flying buttresses built. Many designers find themselves hearing the "sure, it looks good, but. . ." phrase.

Good design is the best solution to a given problem. To have something look good should not be the most important consideration all the time.

AN EASY METHOD TO ACHIEVE GOOD DESIGN.

The different pages of the design section discuss the SAFE design method. This method utilizes a process of design which first sets parameters on and then designs within those parameters.

Let's take the example of a graphic designer who has been employed to design a brochure. If he will set parameters he then can design better and easier. He should ask questions like:
1. What is the budget I have to work within?
2. How much detail do you want within the brochure?
3. Who will read it?
4. What is the setting in which it will be used?
5. What is it supposed to do? Does it sell something, inform, or is it just supposed to look good?
6. Will it be better received by the reader if it is fine art or cartoon?
7. Is it to be read once and then discarded or is it to be retained and referred to on subsequent occasions?

By asking questions a designer can determine the best ways to make his particular design Simple, Appropriate, Functional and Economical.

Think about what questions you would ask if you were to design
1. Some new clothing
2. A new automobile
3. An office interior
4. A filing system for office use
5. **??????????**

Note: Be sure to ask enough questions to help you make the design Simple, Appropriate, Functional and Economical.

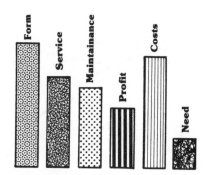

PROBLEM MIX

Design which utilizes a "problem mix" approach is most effective. This problem mix is simply learning to choose the most important to least important aspects of a design. Determine which things are most important and let those things govern your decisions about a problem first.

Every design problem has some areas which are more important than others. Once the different parameters of the design are determined then they are rated according to importance. Using a problem mix approach is like setting priorities. An office chair might need to be designed to:

Look good
Be no bigger than
Be easily movable
Cost less than $_____
Be used behind a certain size desk
Be durable
Be stored easily
Utilize specific colors

And when rated according to consumer importance it becomes much easier to design the very best chair to meet the needs:

1. Look good
2. Be used behind a desk
3. Be easily movable
4. Be Durable
5. Be no bigger than
6. Cost less than $
7. Be stored easily
8. Utilize specific colors

FINDING THE OPTIMUM

Design is finding the best over-all solution. It is considering all the different "needs" of the problem and solving those needs according to importance. Design, like life, is often full of compromises. Good design is the best compromise. It is the optimum solution within a specific set of parameters or boundaries to a given problem.

A good designer learns to optimize. He knows that design depends upon many variables and that he must choose the best solutions. Although good design may last for centuries, most design is as short lived as its need. It is the *best* solution to fulfill certain specific needs.

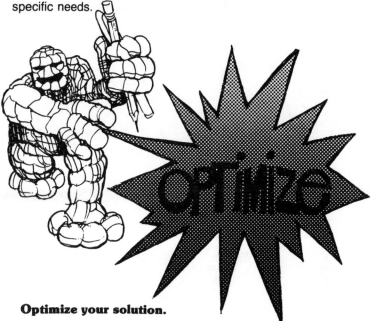

Optimize your solution.

"Before beginning to compose something, gauge the nature and extent of the enterprise and work for a suitable design. Design improves even the simplest structure whether of brick and steel or of prose. You raise a pup tent from one sort of vision, a cathedral from another."

E. B. White

Areas in Design

Design encompasses items from minute detail on one extreme to large and involved undertakings on the other. All aspects of design are inter-related either in function, concept or planning processes. The graphic on these two pages denotes the inter-relationship of design from both ends of the scale. The left represents design as it relates to the

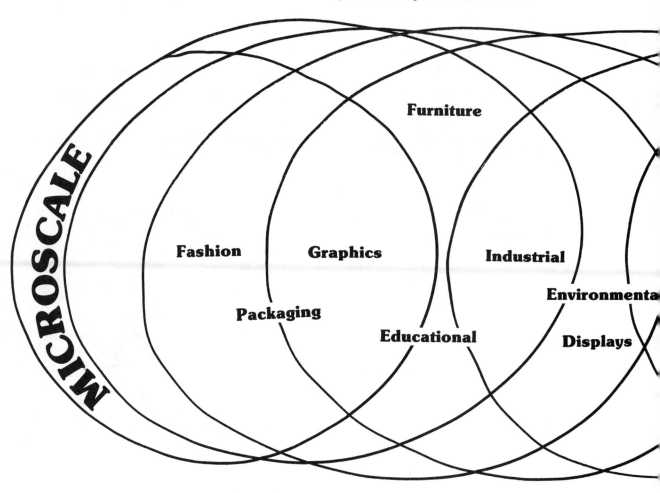

MICROSCALE

Fashion
Graphics
Furniture
Packaging
Industrial
Educational
Environmenta
Displays

**Fashion
Things people
wear**

Clothes
Jewelry
Foot Wear
Hair Style

**Graphics
Things people
read**

Books
Advertisements
Brochures
Posters

**Industrial
Things people
use.**

Tools
Machinery
Instruments
Vehicles

microscale and the right represents the macroscale of design. Illustrations on the bottom help to emphasize the concept—from design as it relates to one person to design as it relates to thousands.

The usefulness of design is limited only by the designer.

The main difference between areas of design is just a change of scale.

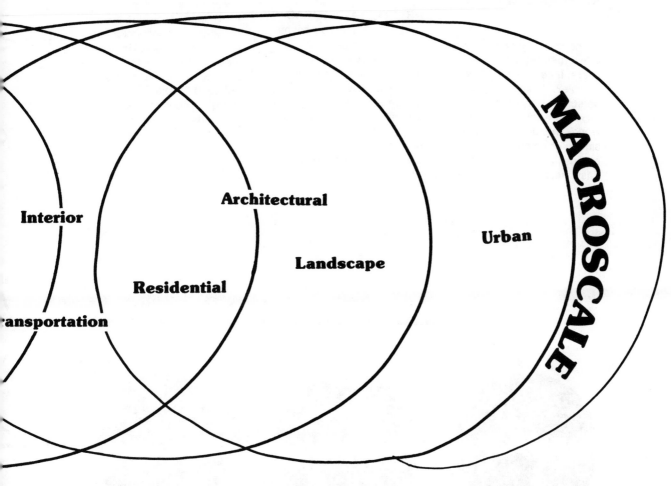

Interior

Architectural

Urban

Landscape

Residential

Transportation

MACROSCALE

**Architecture
Things people
live in**
Homes
Office Buildings
Hospitals
Schools

**Landscape
Architecture
Environment**
Gardens
Yards
City Parks
National Parks

**Urban Design
People living
together**
Community Centers
Cities
Towns
States
Nations

The Design Process

The design process can take a few minutes or several years. It can be simple or complex. It can involve one person or tens of thousands (or even whole nations or worlds indirectly). Whether simple or complex, the design process can be stated in six easy steps:

PROBLEM IDENTIFICATION

This step in the design process identifies design needs and criteria. It generally involves stating problem requirements and limitations as well as gathering and presenting applicable data.

PRELIMINARY IDEAS

The most creative segment of the design process is the idea step. With a good understanding of the identified problem, ideas for solutions are generated. These ideas are initiated by familiar creative steps such as brainstorming, research, survey, or question and answer sessions to provoke the thought processes. Manipulative verbs, bionic comparisons, PAG PAU sessions and synectic sessions (see p. 130) are examples of ways to generate ideas.

DESIGN REFINEMENT

It is at this stage that ideas are examined carefully and are accepted or rejected. Preliminary decisions are made that will influence the rest of the project. The many ideas that have been generated are examined, enlarged or rejected according to their resourcefulness in comparison to the anticipated solutions.

Projection

A designer must always look ahead in the design process. He should temper the design process steps by seeing himself moving toward the approaching end result.

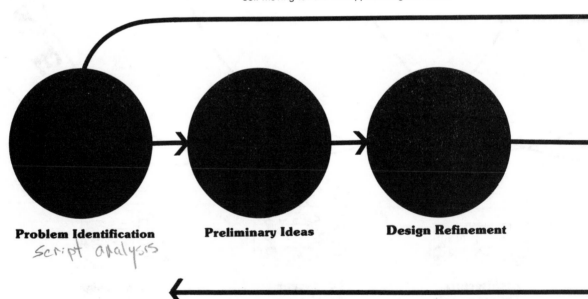

Problem Identification
Script analysis

Preliminary Ideas

Design Refinement

Feedback

Each design teaches new insights which can be applied to future problems. These should be continually re-applied to the process. Experience is a good teacher and a wise pupil is one who can learn from the experiences of others and not waste time duplicating research or mistakes.

ANALYSIS

Careful evaluation and examination of possible idea solutions is conducted. This is the stage when ideas that look good on paper are actually converted into working models for observation. This is when prototypes are made, production problems are analyzed, market research is conducted and human and environmental engineering is compared.

DECISION

Now is the time for an answer. An analysis of the design solution is available at this stage and a decision is made based on the proven results. The design is rejected (and the process starts again), completely accepted or accepted with changes and modifications.

IMPLEMENTION

The End. Final drawings, manufactured products and marketing are the usual fruits of implementation.

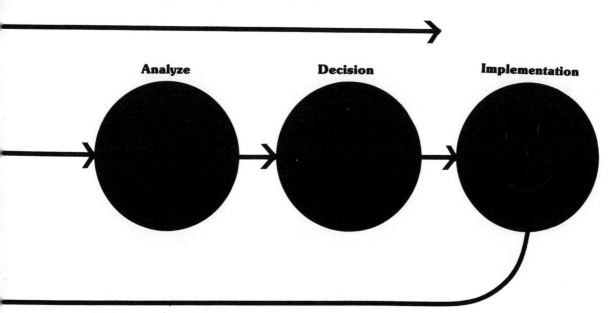

Changes

The design changes with each design problem. You will find that, even though you utilize the six steps of the design process, your process solution will require continual changes. Look for changes and develop your own modified process for each design.

THINKING

Drawing
a way to understanding

Drawing, as seen by most everyone, is a recording of an event, a creative expression. Have you ever stopped to realize that drawing can also be a way of understanding?

We accept graphics as a method of communication. We see blueprints as an essential tool in building communication. We use maps to help us get to places that we are not familiar with. But we often overlook the great value of drawing as a tool to understanding.

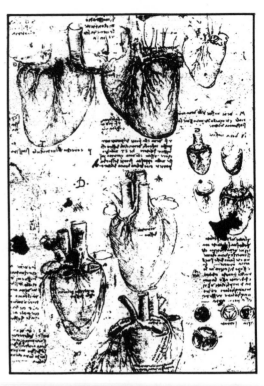

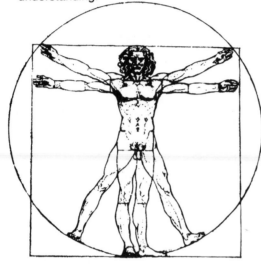

Da Vinci used drawing to help him understand anatomy. Many manufacturers use instruction sheets primarily of drawings to help us assemble the new bicycle or other toy we just bought. Chemists use diagrams of molecular structure to help them understand the microscopic world around us. Sociologists use diagram drawings to help demonstrate the interrelationships of people. And there are many more examples of drawing being used for better understanding. Take a minute and name ten others:

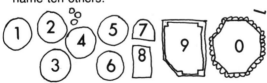

As you have guessed, these next pages deal with drawing as a form of thinking, understanding and communication rather than just expression. Drawing is an extremely useful tool which can benefit everyone. The illustrations demonstrate some of the applications of drawing for better understanding and thinking.

Einstein was able to understand the world of nuclear energy and time relationships because of his ability to visually "see and solve" problems.

64

The abstract principle of interrelationships between individuals takes on new dimension when expressed in the form of a diagram drawing. It is difficult for most individuals who have not been trained in the field of sociology to understand what is meant when social relationships are discussed in verbal terms. Put into pictures, however, it becomes a very simple matter to "see" how it all works and what it all means.

Science has opened many new doors of understanding in recent years. Many of the new discoveries, however, are in areas that cannot be seen, photographed or otherwise visually expressed except through the use of visual metaphors. These visual metaphors, such as the molecular diagram shown below, may not be accurate representations of the actual appearance of molecules, but they are great aids to understanding. Without the use of these imagined visual metaphors it would be almost impossible to understand or communicate to others the relationship of the molecular and nuclear structure of the world we live in. Wouldn't it be sad to think we would have to wait for the invention of a microscope powerful enough to allow us to see the actual structure of molecules before we could begin to draw and understand them? The use of these visual metaphors has opened countless doors to understanding.

Think of the most interesting speaker you have heard recently. Chances are that you remember a speaker that painted visual pictures for you; one that described experiences in detail or helped you to see in your mind a certain experience.

Visual thinking has helped solve some of the most complex and difficult problems of our time. It has allowed us to see medical cures, battlefield strategy, nuclear physics, the relationship of time and light, gravity, and other forces of nature. It is really the foundation of thinking so why shouldn't it be developed as a major basis of understanding for us?

Our educational system has in recent years become convinced of the great value of visual understanding and communication. Movies, slides, diagrams, and many other forms of visual media are standard forms of modern education. We are beginning to believe, and use the fact that we often visually see and understand first and then convert to verbal terms later. This book is an attempt at mixing the visual with the verbal. A picture (drawing, diagram, etc.) is worth a thousand words and always will be because that's the way your mind thinks naturally and easily.

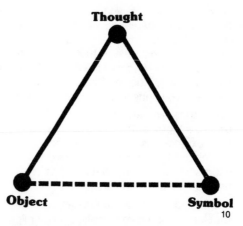

Visual concepts used to understand psychological theories.

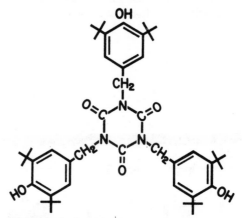

Visuals help explain chemistry.

Visuals are used extensively in electronics.

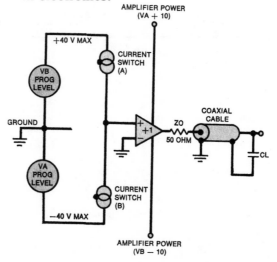

Drawing can help you in many ways. It can be a forced observation tool. To understand about the structure of an orange, draw it. See how it all fits together. Actually, when you draw any item you are forced to closely observe the structure of that object. This careful observation can help you better understand the object.

Drawing can help you even understand people's feelings. If you try to draw people and their expressions you can become aware of the seemingly insignificant differences of expression which are tell-tale signs of the emotional state of the subject.

Drawing can be a great asset in solving problems of creative inventions. You might see something in your mind that would seem workable if built. If you will draw that object in detail before you begin to build it, you can often solve many structural problems before you waste time trying to build it.

Drawing helps you to understand the structure and function of items.

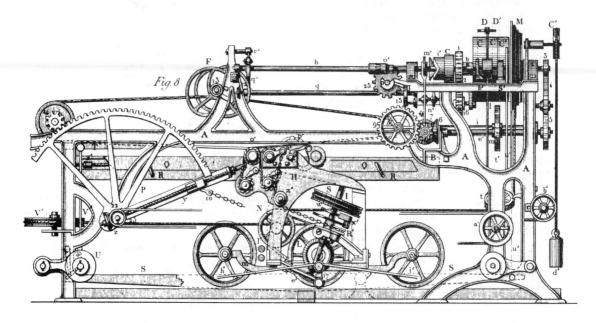

And one last thought: Have you ever stopped to realize that you think in pictures? If you think of going to the store, what comes to mind? It probably isn't the word "store" but is more likely something you can visually see about that store. Maybe you see the outside of the store, aisles inside, a clerk you are familiar with, the shelf or item that you are looking for, or some other thing. If it is most natural for your mind to think visually, doesn't it seem logical that your mind can solve problems and be creative visually. Drawing is a great tool for thinking.

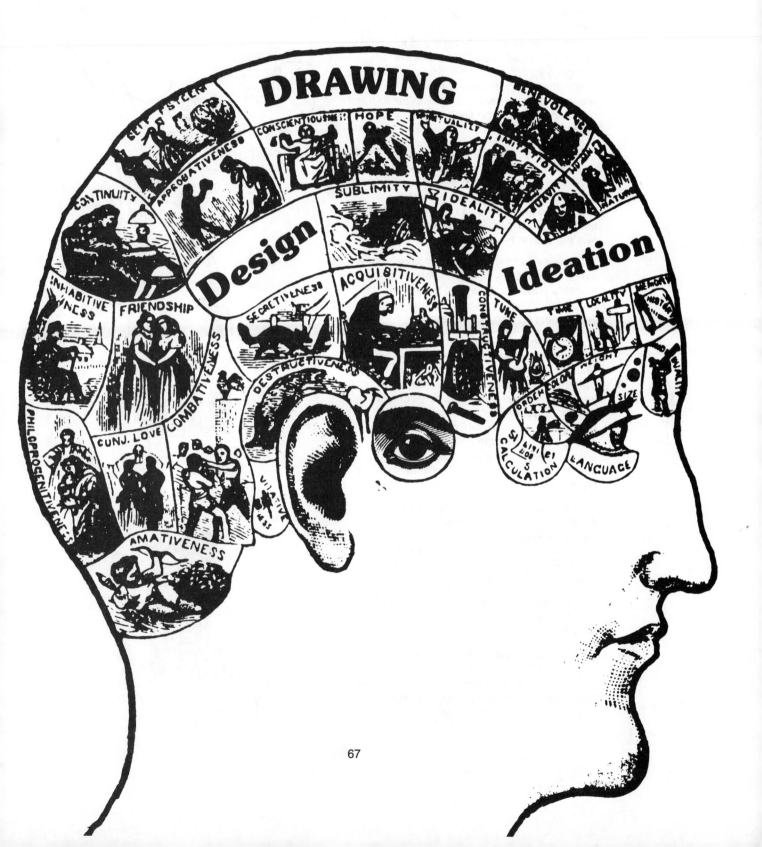

Mental Practice

Mental practice can be used as an aid in designing, public speaking, selling, sports, getting along better with others . . . virtually anything.

One woman once applied mental practice to help her master left-hand driving before touring England and Scotland. In flight and just before falling asleep, she saw herself in a car designed for left-hand drive. She drove the roads, imagining she was coming out of a one-way street, entering into complicated turns or traffic patterns. And she said the system really works.

The late Dr. Charles Mayo recognized the value of mental practice in medicine. Before an important operation, he'd seek a few moments' seclusion and run through the surgical techniques in his mind. He'd mentally wield the scalpel, call for proper instruments, mentally feel the slap in his gloved hand.

Clarence Darrow, the great attorney, often would have his day in court before trial began, mentally playing out his role, forming his argument, weighing its effect on the jury, anticipating his opponent's strategy.

According to Dr. John C. Eccles and Sir Charles Sherrington, experts in brain physiology, *"When you learn anything, a pattern of neutrons forming a chain is set up in your brain tissue. This chain, or electrical pattern, is your brain's method of remembering. So since the subconscious cannot distinguish a real from an imagined experience, perfect mental practice can change, or correct, imperfect electrical patterns grooved there by habitually poor playing."*

Research Quarterly reports an experiment on the effects of mental practice on improving skill in sinking basketball free throws. One group of students actually practiced throwing the ball every day for 20 days, and was scored on the first and last days.

A second group was scored on the first and last days and engaged in no sort of practice between.

A third group was scored on the first day, then spent 20 minutes a day, imagining that they were throwing the ball at the goal. When they "missed" they would imagine that they corrected their aim accordingly.

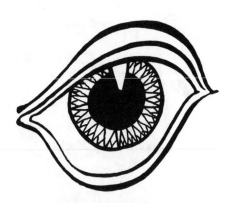

Picture it in your mind's eye.

"First learn how to do whatever you want to do properly through instruction . . . then mentally visualize yourself doing it properly . . . five minutes at a time . . . whenever the time presents itself. Mental practice works."

Earl Nightingale

The first group which actually practiced 20 minutes every day improved in scoring 24%.

The second group, which had no sort of practice, showed no improvement.

The third group, which practiced in their imagination, improved in scoring 23 percent.

Alex Morrison, famous golf instructor and author of *"Better Golf Without Practice,"* enables duffers to chop 10 to 12 strokes from their scores through mental practice. Morrison demonstrates the correct swing and gives a few pointers on the theory of golf. Then he asks the student to spend at least five minutes each day, relaxed in an easy chair, eyes closed, picturing himself on the golf course, playing the game perfectly.

"You must," says Morrison, *"have a clear mental picture of the correct thing before you can do it successfully."* That can be acquired through instruction, by watching championship golf, or, as Gary Player has suggested, by studying action pictures of golfers you admire.

One reason mental practice so often shows a prompt improvement is that, for the first time, instead of struggling to remember many confusing *"do's and don'ts"* you have a complete pattern for performing. Unfortunately, however, unless you continue visualizing, you'll lose this ideal pattern and revert to old, self-defeating ways. Five minutes now can make a difference.
Try it.

11

Before becoming President, Abraham Lincoln imagined what he would say and do as President of the United States.

Visual Thinking —An Attribute of Genius

Albert Einstein was a rare, productive, creative scientist whose unique contributions to theoretical physics were based on an equally unique visual method of conceiving and solving problems.

Details of Albert's early history are lacking, but as far as is known Albert Einstein was the product of a full-term, normal pregnancy and delivery. At birth his mother considered the child's head too large and angular, but in spite of the deformity her doctor said the child would grow well (Sullivan 1972).

Early motor development was normal.

Verbal development was delayed, for Einstein did not speak until age 3 (Holton 1971-1972). His sister Maja (Winteler-Einstein 1924) reports, in her unpublished biography, that his searching for words was laborious and each spoken sentence, no matter how commonplace, was repeated silently with his lips, a practice he was finally able to abandon at age 7. There is no evidence that the child had any trouble eating, chewing, swallowing, or phonating and, although he did not freely associate with his peers, he did have a close and warm relationship with his mother and sister. It seems reasonable, therefore, to tentatively assign the delayed verbal development to some sort of aphasia rather than aphonia or childhood autism.

School work did not go well for young Einstein. Because he had little facility with arithmetic, no special ability in any other academic subject and great difficulty with foreign language, his teacher predicted that *"nothing good"* would come of the boy (Sullivan 1972). Poor performance was not the result of lack of application for he applied himself carefully and diligently, persevering in attempts to do his arithmetic

homework, but more often than not coming up with the wrong answers.

Perhaps it was the frustration of trying so hard and achieving so little that explains his behavioral abnormalities, for he was quick to anger and often violent. Once, at age 5, after he had begun home tutoring and violin lessons, he became so furious at his teacher that he threw a chair at her and gave her such a fright that she refused to see the boy again. In another quarrel, he hurled a heavy bowling ball at his sister, and once, she reports, he tried *"to knock a hole in her head"* with a trowel (Winteler-Einstein 1924). While such acts may not exceed the normal aggressiveness of young boys, it should be noted that behavioral disorders of this type are quite common in the dyslexic and, according to a recognized specialist in childhood learning disorders, these behavioral problems are a common cause for referral of dyslexic children to her practice. With improvement of the learning problem the behavioral disorder usually disappears, and a seeming change in personality toward gentleness and niceness usually occurs. The striking contrast of Einstein's poor behavior as a frustrated child with his remarkable gentleness and sensitivity as an adult suggests that the bad behavior was conditioned by his frustrations, not by his constitution. As his unique skills were recognized and he achieved his distinction as a scientist, the adjustment problems lifted and his behavior changed for the better.

Einstein's verbal disabilities persisted in large part into adult life. His secretary considered him a poor speller, and he once remarked to R.S. Shankland, *"When I read I hear the words. Writing is difficult, and I communicate this way very badly"* (Einstein 1963).

In sharp contrast to his trouble with verbal realms were his abilities in nonverbal spheres of activity. Even before age 10 he was well-known for his construction of intricate and colossal playing-card houses, some of them 14 stories high. Many hours were spent building these card houses and one can only imagine the patience, precision, and thoroughness required, as well as the feeling for spatial relations, balance, and symmetry probably learned in the process. He often completed large jigsaw puzzles, and spent a lot of time constructing buildings from prefabricated blocks.

The extracurricular study of geometry was a special inspiration. Jakob Einstein, his uncle and successful engineer, challenged the boy with geometrical puzzles. When Uncle Jakob demonstrated the Pythagorean Theorem—the sum of the squares of the two sides of a right triangle equals the square of the hypotenuse—Einstein thought the Theorem obviously true from mere visual inspection and in no need of proof. He reasoned this from seeing that *"the acute angle determines the sides"* (Holton 1971-1972, p. 103). Nevertheless, before age 10 he proved the Theorem by a method of his own based on similarities of triangles. This demonstration was different from the orthodox proof, and was probably the first indication that the boy was a creative thinker.

The school at Munich where he did his early studies was word oriented and not equipped practically or philosophically to uncover or develop Einstein's early constructive and visual talents. Learning there was largely by rote. Conceivably, Einstein would have languished forever had he not left that regimented place at age 15 and enrolled in the Kanton School at Aarau 30 miles northwest of Zurich. There is no doubt that this was a fundamental turning point in his life. Aarau school was founded by Pestalozzi, a Swiss educational reformer, who published in 1801 his ideas on visual methods of learning and teaching. Basic to Pestalozzi's

approach was the view that *"conceptual thinking is built on visual understanding; visual understanding is the basis of all knowledge."* An excerpt from his book gives an idea of the approach followed in the schools founded under Pestalozzi's influence:

"I just point out that the ABC of visual understanding is the essential and the only true means of teaching how to judge the shape of all things correctly. Even so, this principle is totally neglected up to now, to the extent of being unknown; whereas hundreds of such means are available for the teaching of numbers and language. This lack of instructional means for the study of visual form should not be viewed as a gap in the education of human knowledge. It is a gap in the very foundation of all knowledge at a point to which the learning of numbers and language must be subordinated. My ABC of visual understanding is designed to remedy this fundamental deficiency of instruction." (1801) 1969, p. 299.

Pestalozzi had a wide influence in those days and even Von Humboldt and Talleyrand visited him and his schools. He freely used maps, diagrams, and other visual materials for instruction. The atmosphere was relaxed and informal. Memorization was discouraged and individual thinking was developed. Each item of learning was carefully linked to a visual base image in accordance with principles described.

At last Einstein flourished in a situation which did not impair the free expression of the particular styles of thinking that were so congenial to him. With the recent organization and partial publication of the Einstein papers (Sullivan 1972), the evidence that this style of thinking was nonverbal and visually mediated cannot be doubted.

Max Wertheimer, a psychologist friend of Einstein, had many opportunities to question the physicist on the concrete events in his

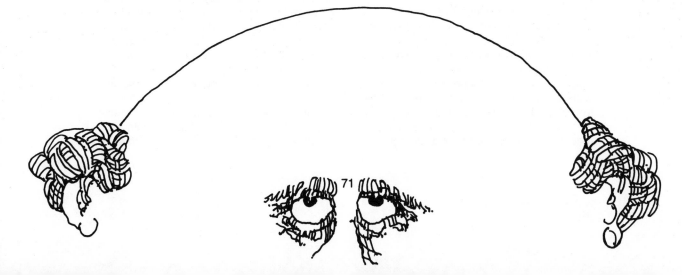

thinking process leading to the relativity theory. Einstein told him: *"Thoughts did not come in any verbal formulation. I very rarely think in words at all. A thought comes, and I may try to express it in words afterwards"* (Wertheimer 1945, p. 184).

Responding to Jacques Hadamard, Einstein again provided an insight into his thought process:

Words or language, as they are written or spoken, do not seem to play any role in my mechanism of thought. The psychical entities which seem to serve as elements in thoughts are certain signs and more or less clear images which can be voluntarily reproduced and combined . . . This combinatory play seems to be the essential feature in productive thought before there is any connection with logical construction in words or other kinds of signs which can be communicated to others . . . Conventional words or other signs have to be sought for laboriously only in a second stage, when the mentioned associative play is sufficiently established and can be reproduced at will (Hadamard 1945, p. 142-143).

Again in his autobiographical notes Einstein emphasized the nonverbal nature of his thought process:

"What precisely, is "thinking?" When at the reception of sense-impressions, memory pictures emerge, this is not yet "thinking." And when such pictures form series, each member of which calls forth another, this, too, is not yet "thinking." When, however, a certain picture turns up in many such series then precisely through such return it becomes an ordering element for such series, in that it connects series which in themselves are unconnected. . . . For me it is not dubious that our thinking goes on for the most part without use of words" (Einstein, 1949, p. 7).

Gerald Holton, professor of physics at Harvard, who worked with the Einstein papers for several years says that an extraordinary kind of visual imagery penetrated Einstein's very thought process (Holton, 1971-72). Holton thinks that the innovative power of this unusual method of thinking was responsible for freeing Einstein from a method of thought that prevented his contemporaries from recognizing the limitations of accepted

concepts of space, time, energy, mass, and light. Other scientists at the turn of the century, according to Holton, *"simply could not make the jump, although their own work prepared the labors of Einstein and others."*

On reading *Relativity, The Special and General Theory,* Einstein's popular book about the origins, implications, and complications of thinking about fundamentals, one is impressed by awkward simplicity and redundancy of Einstein's use of language—especially when contrasted with the splendid visual images he leads us to manipulate in our mind's eye so that we can discover physical truths ourselves. Picturesque thought experiments involving watch readings, light signals, mirrors, positions of locomotives, and lightning are found in abundance. One's understanding of relativity is totally dependent on being able to imagine vividly some thought experiments using mirrors, locomotives, and lightning, and involving the perceptions and reports of two observers moving relative to each other. The style of thinking is completely different from that required in developing a logical, verbal formalism.

Visual images enabled Einstein to clearly understand and manipulate many things. For example, in considering gravity, Einstein asks the reader to imagine a large cage positioned in space. A man is in the cage and the cage is being pulled upward by a large hook at a uniformly accelerating rate. If the man were to let go of a ball in a cage, the ball would appear to fall to the floor and the man in the cage would perceive the fall as the result of a gravitational field operating to accelerate the ball downward. Another observer, looking at the hook from another coordinate system and seeing that the cage was being accelerated upward would see the ball remaining still in space, because of its inertia, and the floor of the cage merely moving up to meet it. In one clear, crisp, clean visual thought experiment Einstein shows us that a so-called gravitational field can be understood in terms of inertia and uniform acceleration. Visual thinking allowed him to scent out whatever was able to lead to fundamentals, and to turn aside everything else that was cluttering the mind and diverting it from the essentials.

After completing his work at the Aarau school Einstein was admitted to the Polytechnical Institute at Zurich. After four years at the "Poly," unable to obtain an academic job such as teaching high school, he took a position at the Patent Office in Berne. It was there, working in his spare time, that he published in 1905 the four papers that revolutionized modern physics: the special theory of relativity, the mass energy equivalence, the theory of Brownian movement, and the photon theory of light including work on the photo-electric effect. His subsequent frame and sojourn at the Institute for Advanced Study in Princeton are well-known. Details of the rest of his life are not relevant to this book but can be found in Phillipp Frank's excellent biography and Professor Einstein's own "Autobiographical Notes" (1949).

At autopsy the brain of Einstein was unremarkable. Sectioning and histological examinations were normal. Detailed measurements of angular, supramarginal, and superior temporal gyri were not made nor was the area of the right planum temporale compared with the left. Such measurements would have been of interest in view of Geschwind's recent findings of increased area of the planum in the dominant hemisphere (Geschwind & Levetsy 1968).

Albert Einstein, it is clear from the record, struggled with a marked disability in verbal thinking and use of language. This is evident from his inability to speak before age 3, his subsequent need to silently repeat words to himself up to age 7, his poor performance in school including his failure in foreign languages in Gymnasium and at the Technical Institute in Zurich, and his laborious and awkward use of language in later life, including the necessity for "hearing words he read." His poor temper control and violent nature during childhood are behaviors common among frustrated children with learning disorders. His extraordinary abilities in construction of card houses, using building blocks, working puzzles, and manipulating geometrical diagrams suggest a specialized mental ability for visual-spatial perception, visual reasoning and visual memory.

The lessons from the Einstein story are clear. The present verbally oriented educational system should include lessons in visual thinking. Children should spend time each day imagining visual concepts or transporting themselves in their mind's eye to different places and seeing another place in their own images of it. For instance, a class of children could be asked to close their eyes and imagine themselves transported to the moon. In their mind's eye they could see the earth over the distant horizon, the vast and lonely lunar craters, the glistening beaded glass on the roughened surface, perhaps American astronauts planting the American flag, and so on. All of these imaginings would more firmly fix the concept on the moon in their minds than would pages and pages of expository prose.

Einstein, of course, was not the only one of our great men who had unusual difficulty with learning verbal skills. Interested readers are referred to Thompson (1971) who presents strong evidence that Edison, Cushing, Wilson, Rodin, and George S. Patton had developmental dyslexia. In these cases a parental figure recognized that the school was wrong in its unfavorable appraisal of the child's intelligence, and either special remedial methods of education at home were adopted or the defect in learning was circumvented by concentration of effort on the development of skills in which the child excelled.

The Einstein story seems to say that under some circumstances verbal thinking may be less useful than visual thinking in solving a particular type of problem. When one drives a car, flies an airplane, or estimates the trajectory of a baseball in order to catch it, words have little to do with the mental process that animates success in these activities.[12]

Original article from *Journal of Learning Disabilities*, Vol. 6, number 7, August-September 1973 entitled "Visually Mediated Thinking: A Report of the Case of Albert Einstein" by Bernard M. Patten, M.D. Edited for this book.

Einstein, A.: "Autobiographical notes." In: P.A. Schlipp (Ed.), *Albert Einstein: Philosopher-Scientist.* Evanston, Ill.,: Library of Living Philosophers, 1949.
Einstein, A.: *Relativity, the Special and General Theory* (16th Ed.). New York: Crown, 1961.
Einstein, A.: "Remarks to Shankland." *Amer. J. Physics*, 1963, 31, 50.
Frank, Phillipp: *Einstein.* Munich, 1949.
Geschwind, N., and Levetsky, W.: "Human brain: left-right asymmetries in temporal speech region." *Science*, July 12, 1968, 161, 186-187.
Hadamard, J.: *The Psychology of Invention in the Mathematical Field.* Princeton, N.J.: Dover Publ., 1945.
Holton, G.: "On trying to understand scientific genius." *Amer. Scholar*, Winter 1971-1972, 41, 95-110.
Luria, A.R.: *The Mind of a Mnemonist: A Little Book About a Vast Memory.* New York: Basic Books, 1968.
Milner, B.: "Memory and the medial temporal regions of the brain." In: K.H. Pribram, and D.E. Broadbent (Eds.), *Biology of Memory.* New York: Academic Press, 1970.
Patten, B.: "The ancient art of memory." *Arch. Neurology*, 1972, 26, 25-31.
Patten, B.: "Modality specific memory disorder in man." *Acta Neurol. Scand.*, 1972, 48, 69-86.
Pestalozzi, J.H.: "Wie Gertrud ihre Kinder lehrt" (Leipzig, 1801). In: Rudolph Arnheim, *Visual Thinking.* Berkeley, Calif., 1969.
Sullivan, W.: "The Einstein papers: childhood showed a gift for the abstract." *New York Times*, p. 1, col. 1, Monday, March 27, 1972.
Talland, G.A., and Waugh, N.C. (Eds.): *The Pathology of Memory.* New York: Academic Press, 1969.
Thompson, L.J.: "Language disabilities in men of eminence." *Journal of Learning Disabilities*, 1971, 4, 34-45.
Wertheimer, M.: *Productive Thinking*, New York: Harper, 1945.
Wertheimer, M.: *Productive Thinking* (Enlarged Ed.). New York: Harper, 1959.
Winteler-Einstein, M.: Untitled unpublished manuscript, 1924.
Yates, F.A.: *The Art of Memory.* Chicago: Univ. of Chicago Press, 1966.
This article from: *Journal of Learning Disabilities*, Vol. 6, number 7, August-September 1973.

VISUAL THINKING EXERCISES

Previous pages discuss the use of visual thinking as practice in better problem solving. In those pages exercises were conducted in the mind to help a person become more proficient at the physical skill he was trying to master. Just as visual thinking can be a help in solving those kinds of problems, it can also be a help in creatively solving problems. These next few pages contain exercises or games which tend to expand the imagination and sharpen our creative thinking.

DAYDREAMING

Daydreaming is a constructive mental exercise. It should, however, be recorded in the personal journal or notebook to be most effective. The journal can contain pictures, designs, poems, words, or just about anything else you want to put in it. It is helpful to take certain time out of each day to daydream. In a classroom situation it can be done by setting aside time for the whole class to put down their heads and daydream. If this is impossible, any 5 to 15-minute period during the day can be used for this purpose.

NIGHT DREAMING

People often find it exciting to discover what their dreams are all about. Indeed, some societies celebrate dream discussion because they have found that the self-esteem of children is raised when they successfully take on the risk of reliving dream adventures. Dreams come and are forgotten quite rapidly.

The following establishes some guidelines to help you obtain more from your night dreaming:
1. Just before you go to sleep, place a journal and pencil near your bed and tell yourself you will awaken when a dream is finished.
2. Go to sleep.
3. After a dream is completed, wake up, and with eyes closed (visual input garbles vision), review the whole dream.
4. Open your eyes and write down the main elements of the dream.
5. Go back to sleep.
6. Next morning, look at your journal notes and elaborate on the dream with particular attention to sensory input—colors, textures, tastes, smells. In either prose or poetry, fill in the detail.

In addition to stimulating your creative thinking, dreaming can be a very efficient way of solving problems that confront you. Many of the world's great thinkers have stated that they "read themselves full and then relax in order to let their mind find the solution." What these men are saying is that they study a problem thoroughly and then they let their mind find the answer. They don't worry about solving a problem . . . they watch their dreams, carefully consider their thoughts and look for any illumination that might hold an answer to their specific problem. Answers often pop up in their dreams, in which case they quickly write down what has occurred to them before it is forgotten again. Learning from dreams works well only if it is recorded immediately and accurately. 13

Note to the reader of this game: Ask your listeners to help you maintain a sensitive reading pace by signaling when they are ready to proceed to the next fantasy (a raised hand or nodded head will do.) Pause at each slash (/) or paragraph for the fantasy to be fully formed by the listeners.

GAME ONE: BREATHING

Let us imagine that we have a goldfish in front of us./ Have the fish swim around./ Have the fish swim into your mouth./ Take a deep breath and have the fish go down into your lungs, into your chest./ Have the fish swim around in there./ Let out your breath and have the fish swim out into the room again.

Now breathe in a lot of tiny goldfish./ Have them swim around in your chest./ Breathe them all out again.

Let's see what kinds of things you can breathe in and out of your chest./ Breathe in a

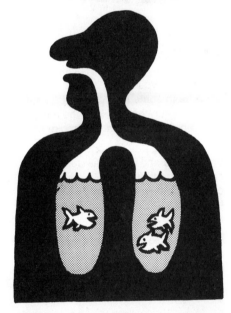

IMAGINATION GAMES

You can put your clothes on or take them off. You can take off a red jacket at the store and put on a green one. But can you change a red jacket into a green one? Or change a cat into a dog? It's easy . . . in your imagination.

These games come from a book by Richard DeMille entitled "Put Your Mother On the Ceiling." The games are fun and stimulate thought.

A right time and place exists to obtain the best results if playing a game. Whenever the participants enjoy the game, the time and place are right. Two conditions will help make it happen.

The first condition is the absence of distraction. It takes concentration to put Mother on the ceiling—at first, anyway.

An even more important condition is the desire to play. Completely involuntary participation may not always be necessary for reading stories or playing checkers but it is indispensable for imagination games. If either player is reluctant, put off playing until later.

lot of rose petals./ Breathe them out again./ Breathe in a lot of water./ Have it gurgling in your chest. Breathe it out again./ Breathe in a lot of dry leaves./ Have them blowing around in your chest./ Breathe them out again./ Breathe in a lot of raindrops./ Have them pattering in your chest./ Breathe them out again./ Breathe in a lot of little firecrackers./ Have them all popping in your chest./ Breathe out the smoke and bits of them that are left./ Breathe in a lot of little lions./ Have them all roaring in your chest./ Breathe them out again.

75

Close your eyes and relax./ Imagine a delicious crisp apple in your hand./ Feel its coolness, weight, firmness, round volume./ Visually see details./ Bruises./ The light reflecting from its bright red surface./ Its many colors./ Now bite the apple./ Hear its crisp crunch./ Smell its frangrance./ Look at the bite and examine what you see./ Oops, some of the juice ran down your chin./ Feel the bite you just took in your stomach./ Feel it being assimilated into your body./ Feel it becoming you!/ Now imagine yourself becoming the apple./ You are hanging in an apple tree./ Take a deep breath and relax./ Let out all tensions./ Imagine, in a very pleasurable way, that you are a beautiful apple in a fantastic clean country setting, in an apple orchard./ Feel the refreshing, cool breeze./ Feel the warm sun on your skin./ It feels good to be part of nature./ Go back in time and become a smaller apple./ Smaller, smaller, greener, tarter yet./ Go back until you become the apple blossom./ Taste the sweet nectar./ Feel the sun on your petals./ Smell the sweet fragrance./ Hear the bees buzzing around you./ Feel yourself as part of nature's growing process involving air, sun, earth, bees, and seasons./ It feels good./ You are a part of nature./ A part of creative unity./ As you return to your aliveness, here and now, you feel good to be a part of nature's creative unity.

14

GAME TWO: CREATIVE NATURE

Breathe in some fire./ Have it burning and crackling in your chest./ Breathe it out again./ Breathe in some logs of wood./ Set fire to them in your chest./ Have them roaring as they burn up./ Breathe out the smoke and ashes.

Have a big tree in front of you./ Breathe fire on the tree and burn it all up./ Have an old castle in front of you./ Breathe fire on the castle and have it fall down./ Have an ocean in front of you./ Breathe fire on the ocean and dry it up.

What would you like to breathe in now?/ All right./ Now what?/ All right./ What would you liketo burn up by breathing fire on it?/ All right./ Continue these until the player runs out of ideas.)

Be a fish./ Be in the ocean./ Breathe the water of the ocean, in and out. How do you like that?/ Be a bird./ Be high in the air./ Breathe in the cold air, in and out./ How do you like that?/ Be a camel./ Be on the desert./ Breathe the hot wind on the desert, in and out./ How does that feel?/ Be an old-fashioned steam locomotive./ Breathe out steam and smoke all over everything./ How is that?/ Be a stone./ Don't breathe./ How do you like that?/ Be a boy (girl)./ Breathe the air of this room in and out./ How do you like that?

What is the name of this game?

Blocks & Bugs

Blocks are mental walls which do not allow people to correctly perceive a problem or conceive its solution.

We all have ways of thinking which cause us difficulty, at times, in perceiving or solving problems. These mental obstacles we shall call blocks.

Once able to recognize these mental "blocks" to problem-solving, we are better prepared to side-step or deviate them. The following are types of common mental blocks which we all experience.

I. The tendency to limit a problem too closely.

Example: Draw four straight lines (without lifting the pencil from the paper) which will cross through all nine dots.

A possible solution is shown on page 78.

A surprising number of people will not exceed the imaginary boundary even though it is not in the stated limits of the problem. The overly strict limits are examples of mental blocks. Expand the mind where limits don't restrict it.

2. Isolating a problem.

Just as common a block is the tendency to overly isolate a problem or to not adequately isolate it. One must learn to isolate the real problems from the apparent ones. An example might be that after many unsuccessful attempts at designing a mechanical tomato picker, someone realized that the answer was not in the machine but in a new tomato plant—a tougher-skinned, more accessible fruit variety.

3. Stereotyping.

Stereotyping is automatically placing value on something—seeing what you expect to see. The example below of a visual "mind-blower" seems awfully strange because of our tendency to stereotype.

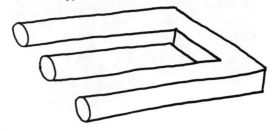

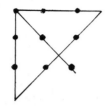

4. Saturation

Saturation is when the mind subconsciously ignores sensory inputs because they are familiar sights. Try to draw a phone dial to prove this one to yourself. Few people can correctly place the numbers and letters on a phone dial. Our mind is so accustomed to the phone that we can't remember what it looks like.

Look at the world upside-down by bending over and looking between your legs. You'll be surprised at how many details are now noticable when looked at from a different perspective.

Creativity may be just a matter of getting rid of something.

5. Failure to utilize sensory inputs.

It is often said that people who are blind have other senses which are enhanced. They can better distinguish by touch, hear better, and smell better. Might it not also be true that people who see rely heavily on vision and partially ignore their other senses?

Bugs

"Bugs" are mental walls created by learned, cultural or environmental standards which do not allow people to correctly or efficiently solve problems.

"Blocks" and "Bugs" are both mental obstacles that hinder us in the solution of problems. "Bugs" are specifically those mental obstacles which we have acquired as a direct influence from the culture that we live in or from the environment that surrounds us. Once we are able to recognize the cultural and environmental bugs that confront us, we then can look past them to find the solution to our design problems. The following are some mind opening examples of "bugs."

1. Taboos

Our society has imposed a set of standards which cause us to act in certain ways in certain situations. These taboos are usually directed against acts which would cause displeasure to certain members of a society. They play a positive role in our society, but can be a hinderance to effective problem solving. Take the example of a family stranded in the desert without water. One very possible benefit of their survival might be collecting urine and sponging their bodies with it to cool themselves and conserve limited body moisture. Documented accounts exist in which families' lives have been saved because of their willingness to consider such action although first impressions were probably negative.

2. Daydreaming

Daydreaming and relaxing are regarded as signs of laziness. This is a common socially imposed standard which is often totally wrong. It has been proven that daydreaming, reflection, mental playfulness and visualizing are aids to creativity, conceptualization, problem solving and accomplishment. This type of "laziness" ought to be considered a positive trait.

3. Intuition and feeling are "bad."

Society often imposes the feeling that judgments and problem solutions should be based on reason, logic, numbers and quantitive information. This information is good and often essential to effective evaluation of a problem, but intuition and "gut-feel" should not be overlooked. Emotion and feelings which are interpreted by intuition are often necessary considerations to solving problems.

4. Tradition opposes change.

Our society, which now highly values innovation, indicates that tradition does not hold the strength it once did. Anything new and different is often met with doubt and skepticism rather than optimism. One should not be so in favor of tradition that he opposes all change or so in favor of change that he disregards all tradition.

5. Assigned cultural and social values.

An example of this might be illustrated in the problem of removing a dollar bill from beneath a precariously balanced object without tipping over the object. It is easy to remove the bill by tearing it in two, but this solution is usually subconsciously ruled out because of our value of money.

6. Environmental blocks.

These are blocks that are imposed by our immediate social and physical environment. The most obvious are physical blocks such as distractions that influence productivity. The physical environment affects everyone.

Yet, because of the individual habit patterns we acquire, different individuals are affected differently.

The "Blocks" and "Bugs" listed on these two pages are by no means all there are. They serve only to introduce to the reader an awareness of how these mental obstacles affect individual production. Look around—be conscious of the almost innumerable and subtle habits, values and environments which influence our lives.

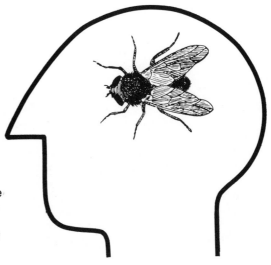

The Numb Man

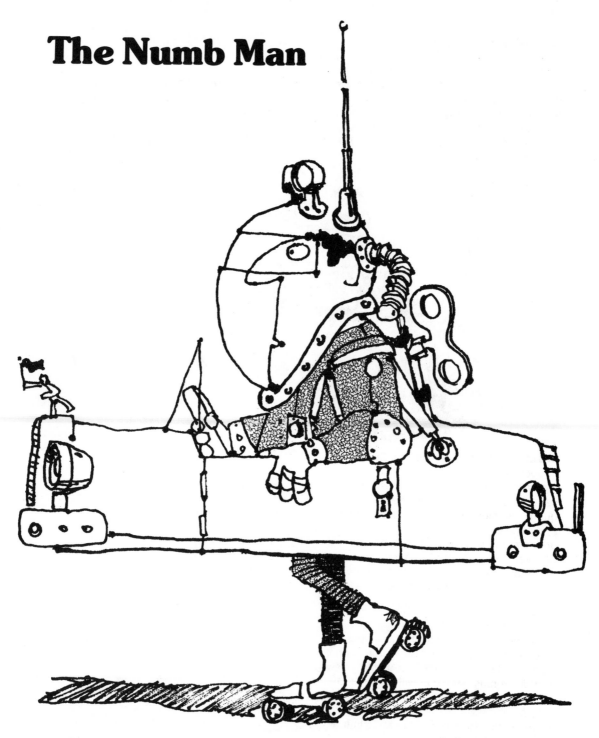

Picture yourself in an air conditioned car. The windows are rolled up, the car is insulated against noise, cold, and heat. You can see out just fine to watch the world around you, but nothing can get in which might affect you. You have no need to do anything but become complacent. You can put yourself in a rut if you like.

Life is just about like that. Many of us become so used to things around us that we shut it all out, just like rolling up the windows of a car.

People often isolate themselves from their surroundings; this makes them set in their ways. Everyone isolates himself from his surroundings to a certain degree—he probably

"Don't wait too long in life to start living." T. Marrow.

Don't become an 82 year-old grunt at age 16. And for that matter don't become a grunt at any age. Don't become set in your ways—numb to the world.

"The tragedy of life is not that we die but is what dies inside a man while he lives." Albert Schweitzer.

needs to in a hectic world—but most of us shut out so much that we become unaware.

Imagine having eyes that cannot see or ears that cannot hear. Imagine having a tongue that cannot taste.

Next time you go to a restaurant to eat notice the speed at which you eat. Probably you eat according to how fast you are served, how much time you have to spend, or whether you are comfortable. Not often do we eat in accordance with how well we like the meal. We eat and taste the food with tastebuds that don't taste or with an attitude that doesn't allow us the opportunity to enjoy what we are doing.

Don't be a numb man. Let your enjoyment of the meal govern how fast you eat . . . at least some of the time.

Get out of your air conditioned car and look at some of the scenery along the road once in a while. You might even find interesting things going on around you in the city, if you notice.

Listen with all your senses.
We need to savor life like a good meal.
If you are ever to become a good designer you must be aware. If you neglect to be aware of the surroundings and forces that act upon you, then you choose to accept a mediocre and tasteless career in design.

Our attitudes about change are governed by our awareness. We all resist change to some degree—maybe we fear it. If we are always aware of a world that is consistantly changing, maybe new, exciting, and different ideas won't frighten us. Change could become fun.

Some of us live in the past, some in the future. But the only real life is now. The past is forever gone, the future always remains in the future.

Here lies Joe's mind it died when he was young

Judgment

Prejudging a situation is another frequently occuring obstacle to progressive, creative or new behavior. How many times have you heard someone say, "You can't do that!" or you say to yourself, "Well, that can't be done so why try?" Judging an idea too early in the problem solving process will cause the rejection of many "good" ideas.

It is essential not to judge too early. Newly formed ideas are fragile and imperfect and they need time to mature and acquire detail before they can be judged adequately. Also, new ideas often lead to other ideas for problem solving. Many techniques of conceptualization, such as brainstorming, depend for their effectiveness on maintaining "way-out" ideas long enough to let them mature and spawn more realistic ideas. It is sometimes difficult to hold on to such ideas because people generally do not want to be suspected of harboring impractical thoughts. One should not judge too quickly!

The judgment of ideas, unfortunately, is an extremely popular and rewarding pastime. One finds more newspaper space devoted to judgment (critic columns, political analysis, editorials) than to creative problem-solving. In the university much scholarship is devoted to judgment, rather than problem-solving. One finds that people who heap negative criticism upon all ideas they encounter are often heralded for their practical sense and sophistication. Negative comments about everyone else's concepts or actions is a cheap way to attempt to demonstrate mental superiority.

Professional problem-solvers have a working understanding of the difficulties of new ideas and respect them, even if they contain flaws. If you are a compulsive idea-judger, you should realize that this is a habit which may exclude ideas from your own mind before they have had time to bear fruit. You are taking little risk (unless you are excluding ideas that could benefit you) and are perhaps feeding your ego somewhat with the thrill of being able to judge others, but you are sacrificing some of your own creative potential.

Analyze an idea or the solution to a problem only after it has gained necessary detail and has matured to a point where it can be fairly judged.

Tags

We have a tendency to label items in our environment with names or tags which limit our understanding or acceptance of the particular item or instance.

Let's look at a very simple example. CAT—means a feline animal to most everyone. Very seldom do we think of the many other things that should be associated with the word CAT. Not only is cat an animal but it also should convey such things as fur, purr, alive, playful, nuisance, expense to feed, meow, nightly prowls, kittens, catching mice, etc.

Problems receive the same treatment of being "tagged" and narrowly considered. How many times have you heard someone comment that a problem was "too hard to solve" or "not worth solving?" Some problems may genuinely be too hard to solve or not worth solving, but all too often they are assumed so without being really evaluated to determine if they are.

Tags are superficial most of the time. You have heard the saying that beauty is only skin deep. The saying invites you to look deeper into a person before just accepting someone as being a beautiful person or a good person. The saying seems to say "beware of not looking deeper into the person."

What about ugliness, on the other hand? Have you ever heard anyone say that ugliness was only skin deep? When you label someone ugly, that's usually as far as it goes. There is no saying which urges you to look deeper into ugliness to find the inner beauty which is often present.

The ironical situation which is created by our treatment of beauty and ugliness is a good example of the superficial nature of tags. In problem-solving, tags don't let you get past the skin of the problem. You are often held at the surface and not allowed to thoroughly examine a problem because of the tags placed on the problem by you or by others.

When a problem presents itself, beware **not** to accept it at face value and pass judgment before examining the situation. You may find that a "problem" isn't a problem after all. A problem to others may be fun to you. A problem to others may be the means for you to become surprisingly wealthy.

We put a rubber stamp on things and there it stays, sometimes forever.

Habits
Habits
Habits
Habits are like having concrete poured into your ear – when it sets you are sunk!

By habits we mean "bad" habits. There definitely are good habits and bad habits, but the generalization here assumes that habits are bad.

Let's look at an example of a new design which was plagued by the habits of people for many years. You have heard of the term "horseless carriage." When the automobile was first invented it was quite appropriately known as a horseless carriage. The inventor conveniently created a self-powered vehicle that looked very much like the already existing carriages. For years people referred to the new automobile as a horseless carriage. It took quite a few years before the first car appeared. People realized after a certain length of time that this new vehicle was not designed for horses and was a completely new method of transportation. Once they began to leave their old concept of "horseless carriages," cars began to appear on the scene. Their appearance changed, their ride changed, the auto was born.

Once accustomed to certain types of behavior it sometimes proves difficult to look at problems from a new angle. We need to leave unwanted habits behind and be willing to look at each new design problem with optimistic vigor.

Habit is a cable: we weave a thread of it each day, and at last we cannot break it.

Horace Mann

Fear, to a certain extent, is beneficial. Something new is a threat to our comfortable "status quo" and therefore produces a certain amount of pressure upon the creator or creative problem-solver. It is a helpful deterrent to really far-out ideas and methods of behavior. Too often, however, any new idea or change is viewed as a threat simply because it is novel. Fear in this instance is a definite obstacle to creativity and progressive behavior. What if the Wright brothers had listened to the people who condemned them for trying to fly . . . an act God meant for birds and not man?

One of the best ways to overcome fear that blocks creative or progressive behavior is to thoroughly assess all the possible negative consequences of an idea. Too often people blithely ignore any consequences, or their general fear of failure causes them to attach excessive importance to any mistake no matter how minor it really is. Often the potentially negative consequences of exposing a creative idea, solving a problem in a somewhat unique way, or taking a daring and progressive step can be easily endured. If one has an idea or a proposed course of action, it is well worth the time to do a brief study of the possible consequences. During the study, one should assume everything will go badly and look at the possible results. By doing this, it will become apparent whether you want to take the risk and pursue the proposed course of action. "Let us not look back in anger or forward in fear, but around in awareness," said James Thurber.

Fear is one of the major blocks to effective problem-solving and creative thinking. Fear of failure, fear of criticism, fear of letting someone down or just fear of trying something new stops many of us from achieving our potential. We have been raised with the idea that if we make a mistake we are punished. When we fail we are often made to realize that we have let someone down. We are taught to live safely (a bird in the hand is worth two in the bush, a penny saved is a penny earned) often to the extent that we become afraid to step out and try something new.

. . .it is better to have tried and blown it than to have never tried at all.

Ima Success

Get It Away From Your Heart

driver murmur to himself about the alternatives available which might free the truck from this awful predicament. After listening for some time, the child decided to offer a suggestion which he had seen others use to free their vehicles. "Why don't you let the air out of the tires and back up?" he asked.

Sometimes we become so attached to problems that confront us that we cannot clearly see the solution. Sometimes we have ideas that are so dear to us that they seem to be great, while if we looked at them objectively, they wouldn't seem so wonderful after all.

Marriage is probably an excellent example of being so close to a problem that it becomes almost impossible to separate yourself from it. And what happens if you begin having marital problems? You go to a marriage counselor. The counselor is professionally trained to look at your problem objectively and recommend action which will help.

There is a story told of a truck driver who was traveling down the highway not really paying attention when all of a sudden his truck came to an abrupt stop. It seems the driver had not noticed a sign which warned of a low overpass. His truck, which was too high for the overpass, had become lodged beneath the bridge. In assessing the situation the driver was undecided what to do in order to dislodge his vehicle. Should he cut the top off the truck, try to pry it loose, drag it out with the help of heavy construction equipment? He looked the situation over for quite a while.

During this whole ordeal a small child had become interested in the situation. He lived nearby and had seen the same thing happen on a prior occasion. He listened to the truck

**Don't marry your problem.
Don't get too attached to your problem.**

SUPERMAN SYNDROME

Many designers have the superman syndrome. They seem to feel that they are the only ones capable of placing a correct value on their superb work. They disregard others' wishes, interests, or interpretation of the work. The superman designer has about a 100% failure rate. Whether designers like it or not, the customer is right at least some of the time.

For anyone who has the superman syndrome a valuable test is offered to establish their true identity. These supermen are asked to leap from a tall building and fly faster than a speeding bullet. If they fly any way but straight down they are a true superman. If they fly straight down—they face about a 100% failure rate.

Excessive pride blurs vision or reality.

The opposite of the superman syndrome is also true. Many designers, artists and other creative people are afraid to act. They feel their work will not be good enough—not up to the standards they want. They are afraid of criticism. They want perfection from the start.

Most important is to produce, to do something. The great masters didn't turn out masterpieces every time. They worked for many years to learn and to finish pieces of art. The great thinkers, designers, and inventors weren't, as a rule, "born with it." They had to try and fail before they were able to succeed.

**Moderation in all things—
not too self confident nor too shy.**

87

PROBLEM SOLVING

Problem Solving

The design process is really a process of creative problem solving. It is a process of constructive, active and, usually, creative behavior.

Solving a problem can be likened to preparing a recipe. A certain mixture of ingredients, prepared in a specific way and cooked for a defined length of time creates a gourmet specialty. These same ingredients, if not treated the same way will not make the same tasty final product And strangely enough the same ingredients, mixed and cooked in different quantities can produce very different but equally delicious results.

The same is true with problem-solving. Each problem is made up of the same kinds of basic ingredients which are evaluated in similar ways and have similar solutions. Each problem and its solution is slightly different, however. It would be unfair and incorrect to imply that one single process or method for solving problems exists. There are as many different ways to solve problems as there are problems and problem-solvers.

The design process is a problem-solving process, but everyone is a problem-solver. Doctor, lawyer, student, housewife, mechanic, musician, writer, boy, girl, or whatever you are, you are a problem-solver. Don't feel like you have to be a designer to benefit from the problem-solving processes discussed here—because after all, remember we are all designers.

All problems, if adequately solved, take the problem-solver on a round trip course a designer normally will go through different stages or energy states until he arrives at the most workable solution to a problem. The design problem-solving process usually takes the designer through the following energy states:

1. Recognize and accept a problem— You must first realize that a problem really does exist and be willing to attempt to correct it. This is a beginning point to problem-solving.

2. Analyze the problem— Get to know the ins and outs of the problem. Discover what the world of the problem looks like.

3. Define the problem— Decide what you believe to be the main issues of the problem. Clarify the major goals to solve the problem.

4. Ideation— Search out all the ways of possibly attaining the major goals. Seek alternatives to solving the problem.

5. Selection— You must select the best possible ways of solving the problem. Choose between the alternatives, trying the most logical solutions first.

6. Implementation— Put into action your selected "best ways."

7. Evaluation— Determine the effect or results of the solution in correcting the problem. Determine the effectiveness of the design.   15

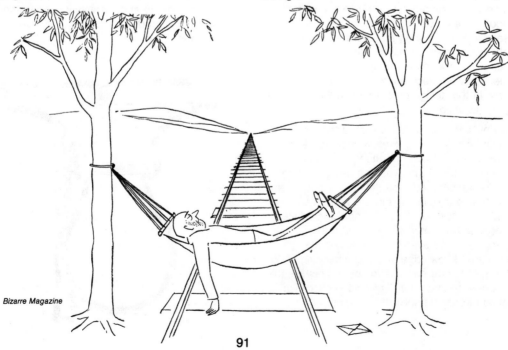

Bizarre Magazine

Some have likened the design process to the process used to generate electricity. Three separate steps dominate the process. First there is the reservoir. Here water is stored before it turns the generators that produce the electricity. During this period of the design process the problem is examined, researched, and the information stored for later use. Next comes the generator. This is when the electricity is actually produced by generators that convert the powers of flowing water into useful electrical current. For design this is the time when the problem solution is decided upon. The goals are set after analyzing, selecting, comparing the information gathered about the many aspects of the problem. The last is the transformer stage. This is when the electricity is directed into useful areas. It is the time in the design process when the goals are put into action.

For electricity to be produced the reservoir must be full—you must fully research and examine the problem at hand. You must know the possible alternatives and have sufficient understanding and knowledge of the problem to choose a suitable solution. If the reservoir isn't full, then electricity will not be produced because the water will not flow to the generators. Likewise, if you don't have sufficient knowledge and understanding about the problem at hand, then you will not be able to draw the necessary information from your mind in order to solve the problem.

The generator must turn and convert the flowing water into electricity through a process of change. The same is true of the design process. You must change the information and understanding of the problem into goals and methods for solving the problem. You must analyze, ideate and creatively change the understanding of the problem into workable solutions.

The transformer is the final link to a usable electrical current. This is the process which directs the current into homes or businesses where it can be used to work for the good of man. In the design process this transforming is the time when the creative thinking and evaluating process ends and the implementation process begins. This is when the ideas and the goals become real through use. This is the actual solution to the problem.

The next pages contain more in-depth explanations of methods for arriving at the solution of a problem. It must be remembered, however, that all problems have their own solution. No two problems are alike and no two solutions can be considered to be exactly alike. The techniques for problem solving and creative thinking discussed in the next pages are like the ingredients in a recipe. They must be mixed and treated in different ways for each problem to produce the delicious solution to the problem at hand.

Many consider the design process and problem solving to be spiral methods of thinking. What this means is that the thinking goes in a spiral and never ending pattern solving one problem after another. Constant research, understanding, goal setting, action, and evaluation form the spiral process of thinking. A designer is forever expanding his understanding of many things, he is constantly setting goals and thinking creatively, and he should always consciously evaluate the results of his efforts.

The best way to become an effective and creative problem-solver is to do it over and over again. The more you practice the better you become. The mind is like a muscle that grows stronger as you use it.

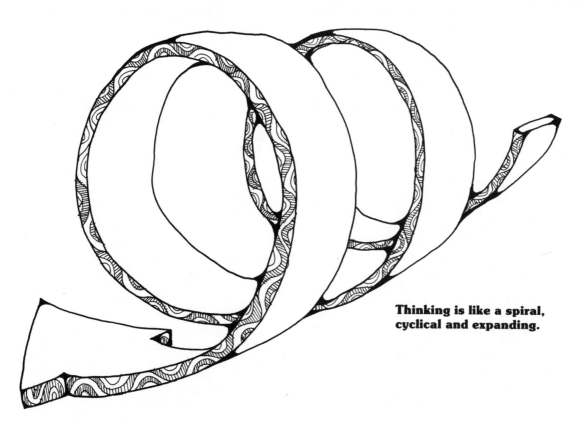

Thinking is like a spiral, cyclical and expanding.

What is the problem

A park ranger was having trouble with motorists speeding around a public park. He set out to resolve the "problem" and make his park a safer place.

What the park ranger had done was to establish "barriers" everywhere. Barriers that reminded the motorists to respect the life and rights and property of others.

Barriers seemed the answer to him. "If I put bumps or dips in the road the motorists will be forced to slow down," he reasoned. And it worked . . . well, sort of. True, the barriers caused the motorists to slow down when crossing them, but the cars immediately sped up after passing.

He would need numerous barriers to stop the thoughtless motorists. That made him think. "It's true I might need barriers to slow down the cars, but why? The motorists drive fast mainly because they don't respect the safety and property of others."

And so he arrived at a workable solution. He bought beautiful tame ducks. The ducks were allowed to roam free, even in the roadways. The motorists were not so inconsiderate as to run over the beautiful birds.

Albert Einstein, one of the world's great thinkers and problem-solvers once said, "The formulation of a problem is far more essential than its solution." What he was saying is that understanding the problem is really the way to solve it. Another great thinker put it this way, "A problem well stated is half solved."

If you know what the problem is, it is much easier to find a solution. All too often people jump to solve a "problem" without really evaluating it. Sometimes we want to remedy the result of the problem, instead of really looking for the problem. We waste much time, expend considerable effort and arrive at only a partial or ineffective solution. It would be much better if we would understand the problem before attempting to find a solution. Some examples might better illustrate the point.

For many years the U.S. Navy had been painting their ships for protection from corrosion. When it came time to order supplies to continue the never-ending ritual of painting a large ship someone asked the question "Why?" "To protect the ship from corrosion from the sea and weather," was the reply. "Maybe there's a better way to cover the ship for protection than painting," was the probable response. The Navy brass put a team of researchers to the test to find a better "covering" to protect the seagoing vessels.

The surprising solution to the new problem was quite different than expected. It was determined that a coating of live algae would best protect the ship's surface. The plant life would adhere to the ship, protect it from corrosive sea water and other elements, and reproduce naturally so one coat would last virtually forever. An old problem seen in a different way produced a better solution.

Most areas in the United States line rivers with sand bags when floods threaten. The sand bags act as levies along the banks to hold the rampaging river in its natural channel. Sand bags are costly, cumbersome, but an effective way of protecting homes and farm lands from flooding rivers.

The Japanese have devised a different solution to the problem. It seems that instead of going to the trouble of locating large amounts of sand to fill sandbags, the Japanese use a more abundant and less expensive filler. They have devised bags which they fill with WATER. These 'water bags' are stacked along the banks of the flooding river the same as sand bags are. They are just as effective at stopping flooding rivers but they are much easier to use. They cost less, store more easily (the water is emptied out) and are easily filled and made ready for use.

It is an excellent solution—somewhat different than the old sand bag approach.

A better solution would probably be to stop the water from flooding or find a good use for the flooding water.

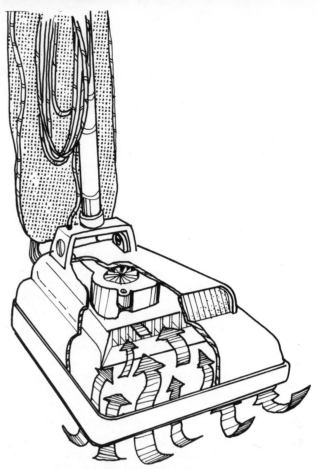

The wind had been blowing dust around for years, but it was not until 1901 that H. C. Booth thought of using the wind in reverse, and thus created the vacuum cleaner to pick up dust.

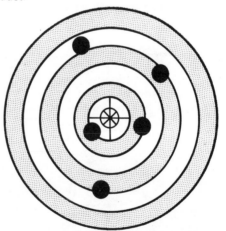

Defining the problem is much like shooting at a bull's eye target. You often know what the approximate problem is you are to solve, just as you know where the target is you are shooting at, but hitting the exact bull's eye is another thing. Sometimes it takes many tries before you are able to zero in on the true problem. Each time you shoot at defining the problem you get closer. After a number of attempts you are able to zero in.

Medical doctors are great examples of problem-solvers. Hundreds of people each week ask them to cure their ills. A doctor will ask questions, probe around a little, ask more questions and run a few tests. Then, after what seems like only a few seconds he tells you what ails your gluteus maximus and how to get better. He writes out a prescription and gives instructions on how to care for yourself.

Doctors are not always correct in their diagnosis the first time, but they are more often correct than incorrect. They use a method of "zeroing in" on the problem. They consider many possibilities in their diagnosis. They consider a number of alternatives before choosing the best answer.

What if a doctor just arbitrarily pescribed a cure? Picture yourself walking into a doctor's office, him looking at you and writing out a prescription. He asks no questions, runs no tests, just arrives quickly at a "well let's try this today" prescription. Would you go back?

As a designer, or any other professional person, your solutions to problems should be at least as thoroughly considered as a doctor's diagnosis. Your designs will be much longer lasting than most cures prescribed by doctors.

If you are asked to design a chair, that chair may be used by millions of people for years and years. If you design safety items for automobiles, you may save thousands of lives.

Thoroughly consider a particular situation to find the correct problem . . . zero in on the bull's eye. Don't let your solutions cause another problem.

"A man without a goal is like shooting a gun without a target."

A doctor does not arbitrarily diagnose a problem or prescribe a cure. He studies, considers the alternatives and chooses the best solution.

FIND THE ESSENCE OF THE PROBLEM

All problems have central themes or major considerations. We call this the essence of the problem. For the park ranger the essence of his problem was to encourage inconsiderate people to respect the rights of others; the Navy needed a covering to protect its boats. You should acquire the skill to be able to zero in on the main problem, to find the essence of the problem.

A doctor questions you about certain symptoms to help him determine the cause of your illness. You need to look at the circumstances surrounding a problem in order to find the essence of the problem. Many times the aspects of a situation are not the problem but are more like the symptoms of an illness. The essence of a problem is like the cause of a physical ailment. You must cure the illness, not the symptoms. You must solve the problem by attacking the essence of the problem and not just the results that a problem has caused.

Ask questions

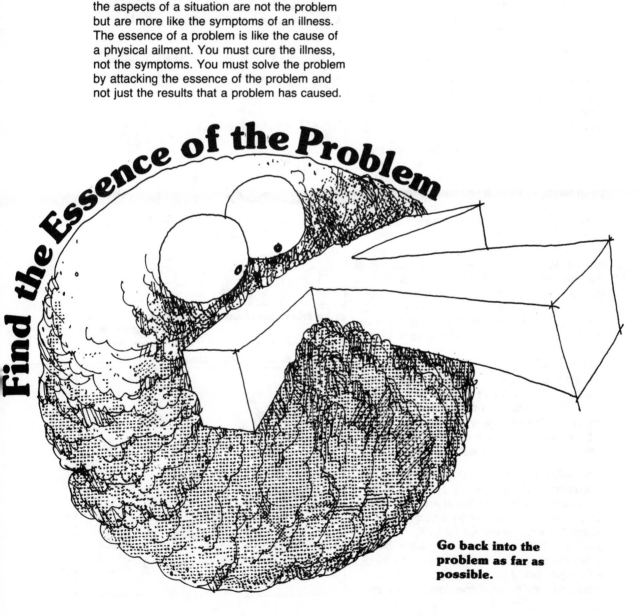

Find the Essence of the Problem

Go back into the problem as far as possible.

Breaking Up Is Easy To Do

A juggler can handle only so much!

Trying to resolve a problem in one bite is tough. But if you'll break that problem up into easily manageable parts it's amazing how easy it becomes.

Remember the last English theme you had to write? What a job! But if you'd broken that same assignment into small parts it would have been relatively easy. If you had looked at the theme as—1. gathering the materials such as paper, pencil, etc. 2. choosing a topic 3. researching the information 4. choosing the most pertinent facts for your theme 5. outlining the theme to determine the general direction of your writing 6. writing the first rough draft of the theme 7. writing the final finished copy to be handed in—it would have been a different job. It is easy to put off writing the theme, but if you do it a little at a time it doesn't seem like quite such a big job. It isn't hard to gather the materials and sharpen the pencils. It isn't difficult to choose an interesting topic and read about it. It isn't difficult to complete a theme when taken a step at a time. Solving any problem is the same way. When taken a part at a time it is usually much easier to obtain a workable solution to almost any problem.

Visualize yourself as a juggler when solving a problem. If you are tossing around one or two aspects of that problem at a time it is quite simple. A juggler can handle a couple of balls easily, but what happens if he gets overloaded? He drops everything when he tries to handle too much. You'll do the same thing with a problem. If you take on too big a problem or too much at one time, you'll bomb

If he overloads

OUCH!

If he tries too many, he ends up dropping them all.

Combine the pieces into manageable parts to more easily solve problems.

out and drop the whole shebang. But if you can cut that problem into manageable pieces you can solve it easily.

Solving a problem is like eating a delicious pie. Try to eat that whole pie at one time and see what happens. The only way you'll enjoy your pie is to eat it a piece at a time. Each piece must be big enough to give you an ample taste of the pie, but not so big as to choke you.

Problems should be divided into primary, functional needs. That is to say they should be divided into related parts with the same basic function. Trying to understand what a problem is all about is a primary functional need. Determining a workable solution after having given it much thought is another primary division. Putting the solution into practice is a third primary division.

At the beginning of the problem solving section we talked about the seven energy states of a problem. These are the primary functional needs that must be met to solve most all problems. Go back to the first page of this section and read those seven energy states again. See if 1. recognizing and accepting a problem, 2. understanding the problem, 3. analyzing and defining a problem, 4. ideation, 5. selection, 6. implementation, 7. evaluation, seem like reasonable divisions of a problem to help make an easy solution.

Remember— Breaking up is easy to do!

Information

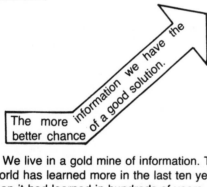

You cannot solve problems without some background knowledge. Even "spur of the moment solutions" are based on some fact. The more knowledge or background, the better the solution to a problem. Remember, the solution of one problem shouldn't create another.

How do you get the information essential to planning the solution to a problem? First, there are basic questions you can ask or basic checklists you can apply against your specific problem (you will find a variety of different helpful checklists in this section on pages 110-113). Second is that you should acquire a working knowledge within the area of your problem. The more reading you do, the more knowledge you will have to help you on a given subject. Be inquisitive. Take things apart. Ask questions.

The more information we have the better chance of a good solution.

We live in a gold mine of information. The world has learned more in the last ten years than it had learned in hundreds of years preceding. Even more exciting is that we have access to our newfound wealth of knowledge. The world is publishing books, movies, video tapes, magnetic tapes and microfilm at a fantastic rate. No one could ever keep up with all that is being published, but if he could just keep up with how to find it he could solve almost any problem.

Probably the best way to gather information is to ask the librarian. You don't need to know all the information in the library, but you do need to know how to find what is in the library. If you become friendly with the librarian he or she will be able to help you find what you need. Or better yet, if you become familiar with the library itself then you will be able to find the answers you need.

It has taken many years of research and study, but it is now conclusively proven that you can't drink from a dry well. If you want to have information to draw from for the solutions of the problems then you will need to go to the library and learn how to use that library. You will need to "fill your head with some facts" before you can "drink from the fountain of knowledge." Information doesn't just come spontaneously, it comes from somewhere. If you don't work to fill your mind with background information, when it comes to solving a problem you will face a "dry well" of information.

At the same time, you won't be able to learn about everything. Everybody is ignorant to some degree. In other words, go to the experts in specific fields and let them help you solve the problems.

Keep an open mind, learn from others, read and listen, try new things, experience.

One efficient method often used is to create a file of information on a variety of subjects. You will find that the little odds and ends facts that you learn, if filed in a place where you will be able to find them again, can be very useful. You will save yourself much time and effort by making your own filing system to help you remember the things you learn.

You can't drink from an empty bucket!

Values

The previous page talked about gathering information. Equally important as gathering the information is the ability to distinguish the value of the information gathered. Much information will be useful and much of it will be worthless in the solution of a specific problem.

Too often designers overlook their influence on the final judgment of the design. They decide if the final product is good or bad. They have no one to blame if the end product is not acceptable or workable because they are the ones that created the final result. Their judgment information is equally as influential. If designers don't learn correct value judgment their information-gathering and problem-solving will be useless.

The most important concept when valuing information or ideas is to relate it as closely as possible to true face. Don't assume too much. Because John married Jane does not necessarily mean that they love each other. They may live in a country where the custom is for the parents to arrange marriages. The only fact is that John married Jane. As you investigate the circumstances you may find other facts, but given the information you have here, the only fact you can correctly assume is that they are married to each other.

A test of the value of information is to determine how relevant the information is when converted into action. If the information is useful to the solution of a problem, then it has a high value. Establishing a priority list of the usefulness of information helps determine its value. Take information gathered and rate it as to usefulness. The chart below shows the priority rating of information gathered about the design of a new car.

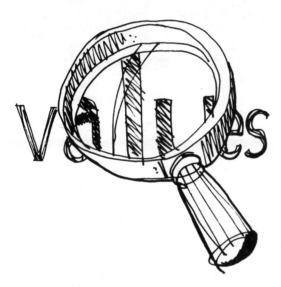

Factual information is essential to the proper solution of a problem, but equally important is the value or interpretation of that information. For instance: an earthquake is a terrible thing. If you are able to witness an earthquake on television or in a movie it is interesting and maybe frightening, but certainly not as terrible as it was to those who experienced it. If you are becoming informed, as you receive accounts of the earthquake you will need to distinguish the value of that information according to the informant who reports it to you.

Values are relative one to another. A flood to an ant is but a trickle of water to you. A frightening airplane ride to you is boring to a daredevil pilot.

How to evaluate the information is probably as important as how much information you get.

Priority Lists

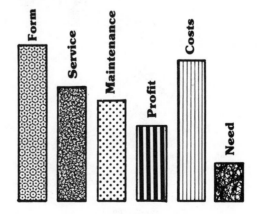

Design a Method to Solve Your Problem

Problems are an everyday fact of life. We are constantly confronted with problems. Some are serious, but most are simple. Let's take a look at some of the methods used to solve problems.

Many solutions or methods of solving problems are overlooked simply because they are common. Some of these problem-solving techniques have valuable lessons to teach.

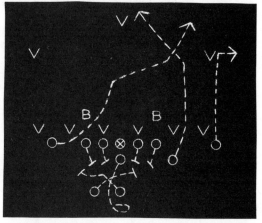

Take your favorite weekly sports event for example. The team and the coach that you enjoy watching so much go to considerable effort to win each game. They consider games to be major problems or obstacles in their path to a winning season. They spend many hours plotting the plays they use and attempting to establish an effective defense.

One of the most helpful methods they use is to plot on game plan charts the plays they run. This visual diagram enables them to coordinate efforts between players. All players are able to see their role in a play that is planned for the next game. It is a great problem-solving technique.

What about using that same principle of plotting "game plans" for other kinds of problems? Maybe you could plot certain courses of action to help you through a problem. Can you think where a plotted course of action could have helped you solve a problem more easily in the past? Just for fun, let's look at other examples of how visual "game plans" or problem-solving methods are used for other types of problems.

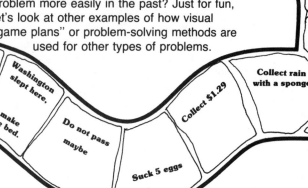

Do not pass
Jail

Start, restart. Reset go.

Collect with a sponge
Winnie pood.

Wipe off your feet.

Old ironsides has wooden sides.

Go directly do something new.

Washington slept here, make the bed.

Do not pass maybe

Suck 5 eggs

Collect $1.29

Collect rain with a sponge.

Think of the game of WAR, red and blue army games, people and nations have played since the beginning of time. War is often manipulated much the way a football or baseball game is. War leaders gather around maps or blackboards and plot courses of action that their soldiers will take against the enemy. These meetings produce plans of action which can be used to eliminate the enemy or problem.

There're as many methods of solving problems as there are problems.

We're tired of doing these things.

Suck 5 eggs

CABLE CARS of San Francisco, Calif. THE ONLY OFFICIAL NATIONAL MONUMENT THAT MOVES

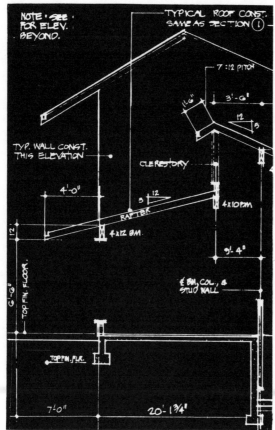

Suppose you had to tell a girl or boy friend that you were no longer going out with each other. You could tell your 'steady' directly. You could tell their brother or sister who could break it to them gently. You could tell a good mutual friend and have them slip it to them. What you are doing in all this is attempting to establish some plan to solve your problem. After considering the problem and the alternatives you arrive at a workable plan.

Now what does all this talk of planned solutions to problems mean to you? Simply that if you will plan ways to solve your problems, you will be able to solve them easier, faster, and much better.

As you have seen from the previous paragraphs, problems can be solved in many different ways. Each problem has its own solution. Learning to use different approaches will greatly help you to become a better designer and problem-solver.

Plan your work
Work your plan

Have you ever looked at a blueprint? Aren't blueprints really just methods of solving problems? Blueprints are visual plans for building a house or other structure in the most efficient and best way. If you don't think blueprints are methods to solve problems just think of all the trouble that would develop if you tried to build a house without them.

The last English theme, business memo, or research report you wrote probably started with an outline, a rough draft and finally the finished product. These are planned methods of solving a problem. You utilized a step-by-step approach to arrive at a finished copy to fulfill your needs.

Look at the problem
Develop a plan to solve it
Work at the plan
Evaluate your plan

IDEATION

Ideation

IDEATION IS THE PROCESS OF GETTING GOOD IDEAS

Good ideas are available to everyone. You've probably had good ideas and will undoubtedly have more. All ideas aren't as momentous as Edison's light bulb, Bell's telephone, or Morse's telegraph, but everyone has excellent ideas to meet his individual needs or problems.

In 1920 it was determined at a conference on patents that very few inventions were left to produce. They decided all the good ideas had already been expressed and so they wouldn't be issuing many more new patents. It is fortunate that inventors of the television, jet engine, life saving medical machinery, transistors, etc. weren't at that conference. The truth of the matter is that new ideas will continue as long as men are upon the earth.

You may as well get on the band wagon. Try having a few new and creative ideas—you may be surprised.

You may know a person who seems extremely creative to you. For some reason, this person has one idea after another. Wouldn't it be convenient to be able to command new ideas to come just as your creative friend seems to?

This section of the book deals with ideation—the practice of obtaining ideas. It is true many ideas just happen, but many other ideas are made to happen. Creative ideas aren't limited to gifted people.

An idea is the first step to anything. This book was once an idea in the minds of the authors. Now you've got a book.

Edison had an idea it would be possible to record sounds which could later be reproduced. This idea led to the phonograph.

The next pages talk of different methods of obtaining creative ideas. Unfortunately there are as many creative thinking or idea-getting processes as there are ideas. Fortunately most idea-thought methods involve analogies of one type or another. The next pages tell how to get ideas over and over again by employing analogous thinking processes.

Once you have good ideas, don't be afraid and horde them. If the world had all the good ideas that were never developed, it would be a much different place. Stories circulate of good ideas that were stolen from inventors by dishonest businessmen. It is wise to be selective with a good idea but never selective to the point it isn't developed. It is better to give out ten ideas that will help mankind and personally profit by only one than to hold all ten and let no one profit at all.

LOOK for creative ideas. This is the first secret to obtaining new ideas. Seek and ye shall find!

It takes courage to be creative, just as soon as you have a new idea, you're in the minority of one.
E. Paul Torrance

Brainstorming

Small children seem to be the most creative people in the world. They'll try anything new. Their experiences are so limited that their minds run rampant with creative new ideas. They don't let anything get in the way of their creative thoughts. They don't judge thoughts, they don't restrain thoughts, they don't discard thoughts—they just think.

"The way to have a good idea is to have lots of ideas," said a great scientist. Children have lots of good ideas.

As we get older, it seems that we often become less creative and daring. As children we exercised our imaginations freely, but as we grow up we each become more sophisticated

and less free. Schools teach us to look for the "right answers." Perceptual, emotional, cultural or other conceptual "blocks" limit our free flow of ideas; fear of being "wrong" or "different" causes us to prematurely disregard or ignore creative thoughts that enlighten our minds. But there is a way to be creatively rejuvenated again—BRAINSTORMING is the answer.

WHAT IS BRAINSTORMING?

A Brainstorming Session involves a gathering of two or more people to explore creative ideas about a subject and is a session where people exchange a number of ideas which in turn stimulate them to think of more ideas. An idea from one person stimulates wild responses from another which in turn stimulates more and more and more creative reactions. A brainstorming session should be like an explosion of thought.

How do you Brainstorm?
The following is a simple method to more than double your creative capacity:

16

First pick a subject or problem, then apply the following principles.

1. THINK FIRST — JUDGE LATER!

Sound simple? It is. By letting your mind run wild you can eliminate all "blocks." Don't judge what you think; if you are in a group don't hold back an idea, just let it out. Don't say to yourself, "I won't say that because they'll think I'm stupid" — don't hold back any ideas. If you are brainstorming by yourself, write down on a piece of paper EVERYTHING that comes to your mind concerning the subject.

REMEMBER—DON'T JUDGE. We want QUANTITY not QUALITY of ideas.

2. THE WILDER THE IDEAS THE BETTER

Let your mind get out of its everyday way of thinking. Let it be creative. Off-beat and impractical ideas often "trigger" other ideas which can be very useful.

3. QUANTITY IS WANTED

The greater the number of ideas the better the chance of having a winner. It is easy after a Brainstorming session to eliminate useless or ridiculous ideas. It is extremely difficult to "puff-up" a short list of ideas. Without the QUANTITY, you'll most likely not find the QUALITY ideas either.

4. COMBINE, IMPROVE, AND EXPAND IDEAS

Suggestions of how to improve the ideas of others is welcome. Carry any idea a little further and make it a little better. Look for ways to combine two or more ideas to make an even better idea.

5. TAKE SHORT RECESSES OR BREAKS

Let your mind mull over the ideas while you take a walk or get a drink. When you relax and let your mind go to work, the new ideas that will just pop into sight, seemingly from nowhere, will surprise you. Most of us have accidentally experienced illumination after having worked on a problem to the point of frustration. It is amazing what answers the "inner mind" will spew forth when left alone to work. Use all of your mind, not just the tip of it.

6. EVALUATE YOUR IDEAS

After you have obtained a long list of ideas, after you considered available information pertinent to your problem and after you have allowed your "inner mind" to give even greater illumination, then evaluate what has happened. This is the step where you judge the quality of your ideas.

7. DO SOMETHING ABOUT IT.

Put your ideas to work. Brainstorming is the beginning of worthwhile ideas that later are put into use.

Reason can answer questions, but imagination has to ask them.
Ralph N. Gerard

Originality is simply a fresh pair of eyes.
Woodrow Wilson

Almost all really new ideas have a certain aspect of foolishness when they are first produced.
Alfred N. Whitehead

No idea is so outlandish that it should not be considered with a searching but at the same time a steady eye.
W. Churchill

Lists

Many people use checklists when shopping to help them quickly and accurately buy all the goods they want. Can you imagine how many times one might have to go up and down aisles in a large department store when shopping for specific goods if he didn't have a list to remind him and simplify his trip to the store? Checklists are a good way of solving problems.

THE CREATIVE PROBLEM SOLVING PROCESS

Find a Problem

Examine and get to know the problem

Define the parameters to get a handle.

Generate ideas or possible answers.

Select the best idea.

Try it out.

Evaluate to see if it worked.

Problem Finding / Sensitivity to Challenges

Friends?	Social Life?
Family?	Transportation?
Neighbors?	Social Life?
Church?	Personality?
House?	Leisure Time?
School?	Money?
Homework?	Plans and Goals?
Graduation?	Hopes and Desires?
Bottlenecks?	Routine?
Anxieties?	Pet Peeves?
Performance?	Appearance?
Career?	Improvements?
Happiness?	Comfort?
Misunderstandings?	Complications?
Waste?	Inefficiencies?
Attitudes?	Safety?

Fact Finding / Descriptive Catagories

OBJECTS

Function	Texture	Time
Structure	Odor	Space
Substance	Sound	Color
Taste	Shape	Magnitude

SITUATIONS

Who?	When?	Why?
What?	Where?	How?

Problem Need Checklist

Which of the needs are
  vital?
  very important? Why?
  important?
  desirable?
  unimportant?

What are the needs of
  the functional system?
  the user?
  the company?
  the outside world?

What are the needs at each
of the ten product life stages?
    1.Designing & drawing?
    2.Development?
    3.Production of components?
    4.Assembly?
    5.Testing & adjusting?
    6.Finishing & packaging?
    7.Distribution?
    8.Installation?
    9.Usage & mis-usage?
    10.Maintenance & servicing?

LOCATE NEEDS ACCORDING TO
IMPORTANCE

Who's important?

Why are they important?

Identify And Analyze The Main Need

(The Main Need is the need that if not properly
satisfied makes the fulfillment of all the other
needs pointless.)

Idea Finding / Spurring Questions

Put to other uses?	Modify?
Substitute?	Minify?
Rearrange?	Reverse?
Adapt?	Combine?

Applied Imagination Checklist

PUT TO OTHER USES?

New ways to use as is? Other uses if
modified?
Adapt?
  What else is like this? What other idea does
  this suggest? Does the past offer a parallel?
  What could I copy? Whom could I emulate?
Modify?
  New twist? Change meaning, color, motion,
  sound, odor, form, shape? Other changes?
Magnify?
  What to add? More time? Greater
  frequency? Stronger? Higher? Longer?
  Thicker? Extra value? Plus ingredient?
  Duplicate? Multiply? Exaggerate?
Minify?
  What to subtract? Smaller? Condensed?
  Miniature? Lower? Shorter? Lighter? Omit?
  Streamline? Split up? Understate?
Substitute?
  Who else instead? What else instead? Other
  ingredient? Other material? Other process?
  Other power? Other place? Other approach?
  Other tone of voice?
Rearrange?
  Interchange components? Other pattern?
  Other layout? Other sequence? Transpose
  cause and effect? Change pace? Change
  schedule?
Reverse?
  Transpose positive and negative? How about
  opposites? Turn it backward? Turn it upside
  down? Reverse roles? Change shoes?
  Turntables? Turn other cheek?
Combine?
  How about a blend, an alloy, an assortment,
  an ensemble? Combine units? Combine
  purposes? Combine appeals? Combine
  ideas?

Five Characteristics of the Creative Thought Process

1. Transportation 2. Disorder 3. Intuition
4. Incubation 5. Sequence development

Manipulative Verbs

Multiply	Divide	Eliminate
Subdue	Invert	Separate
Transpose	Unify	Search
Delay	Distort	Rotate
Flatten	Squeeze	Complement
Submerge	Freeze	Soften
Weigh	Destroy	Concentrate
Fluff-up	By-pass	Add
Subtract	Lighten	Repeat
Thicken	Stretch	Adapt
Relate	Extrude	Repel
Protect	Segregate	Integrate
Symbolize	Abstract	Dissect

Searching Checklist

What can be learned by asking the six
fundamental questions?
What has to be done? (Needs)
Why has it to be done? (Reason)
When has it to be done? (Time)
Where has it to be done? (Place)
By whom or what has it to be done? (Means)
How has it to be done? (Method)

Intended to generate a variety of design alternatives

How can each part of the design be:
Eliminated?
Combined?
Standardized?
Transferred?
Modified?
Simplified?

Option Checklist

DECISION OPTIONS
Recognize need
Recognize inevitable element
Imagine decision
Tentative decision
Firm decision
Cancel decision

JUDGMENT OPTIONS
Assume
Weigh
Weigh & compare
Extrapolate
No further action
Predict

STRATEGIC OPTIONS
Continue in same direction
Continue plus increment
Change direction
Back check
Advance check
Scan
Resolve conflict
Continue with increased effort
Recall

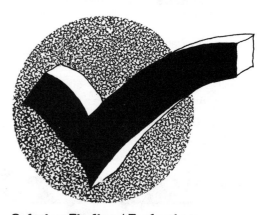

Solution Finding / Evaluation

Effect on objective?
Individual and/or groups affected?
Cost involved?
Tangibles involved (materials, equipment,
    etc.)?
Intangibles involved (opinions, attitudes,
    feelings, aesthetic values, etc.)?
Moral or legal implications?
New Problems causes?
Difficulties of implementation and follow up?
Repercussions of failure?
Timeliness?

Acceptance Finding/Implementation

Acceptance: In what way might I gain acceptance?

Anticipation: How might I overcome anticipated objections?

Assistance: In what ways might other persons or groups help me?

Locations: What places or locations might be advantageous?

Timing: In what ways might I use special times, dates, etc?

Precautions? What measures might test my "best" idea?

CONCEPT OPTIONS
Use concept
Change plans of abstraction
Use outline strategy
Change viewpoint
Compare with existing system
Compare with emerging system
Apply primary roulette
Apply secondary roulette

OBSTACLE OPTIONS
By-pass obstacle
Destroy obstacle
Remove obstacle
Start over with new actions
Start with new actions from decision
Actions in one, two, thee, or more dimensions

TACTICAL OPTIONS
Assess risk
Check consequences
Develop
Compare with another decision
Divide action
Adapt another decision
Concentrate on small area
Factor
Check cause
Question further decision
Reverse decision
Try alternatives

RELATIONAL OPTIONS
Store decision
Expose decision
Delay decision
Communicate decision
Relate to previous decision
Search for redundancy
Search for inadequacy

17

Ah-Ha is the feeling of having received an insight to a problem that has been bothering you for some time . . . a problem that you've been unable to solve.

An excellent example of the Ah-Ha principle is Newton and the apple. When asked how he came to understand gravity Newton answered, "By thinking about it all the time." He had been pondering the problem for quite some time. Then, one day while sitting under an apple tree, the concept of gravity came to him when he saw an apple fall.

Many people laugh and say that it is obvious to know gravity exists when you see an apple fall. But that isn't what Newton saw at all. What he saw was the existence of strong attracting forces that caused the apple to fall. The mathematical formulas and complexity of the theory of gravity developed by Newton are thoroughly understood by relatively few people.

Another example is Darwin. He tells the story of walking down the road when the theory of evolution came to him. He can describe the exact spot in the road where the idea "struck" him.

You probably have had the same type of an experience as have these two great thinkers. Methods exist which can help you become more receptive to this kind of "idea getting."

YOU HAVE TO HAVE SOMETHING TO THINK ABOUT AND YOU HAVE TO HAVE SOMETHING TO THINK WITH. GIVEN THESE TWO, LET YOUR MIND SOLVE THE PROBLEM.

THE SPONGE, THE EGG and THE IDEA

The following is a discussion of a technique for getting the Ah-Ha! principle to happen more often in your life.

As you set about solving a problem that's bothering you, make your mind into a sponge. Let your mind soak up all the information pertaining to the problem and various possibilities that it can. This process should cover some period of time, depending upon the complexity and seriousness of the problem.

The sponge phase of the Ah-Ha principle gives your mind the raw material it needs to work with. During the sponge phase you're concerned only with input—not answers. You should turn the problem over and over and look at it from every possible angle and direction. Consider every possible solution or idea that might have any bearing on solving the problem. Study it, read any books you might find on the subject, talk to knowledgeable people about it to absorb their ideas. Pack everything you can into your mind until you reach a saturation point.

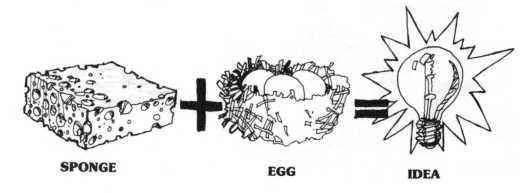

SPONGE   **EGG**   **IDEA**

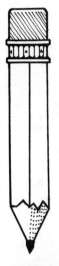

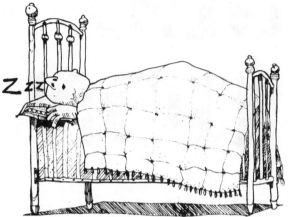

WHEN YOU HAVE AN IDEA WRITE IT DOWN

Now the EGG! Let your mind incubate the information and the problem that has been before you. Turn to other things and leave the problem alone. Put the things out of your mind by going fishing, concentrating on other things, riding a dog, whatever.

To enter into the egg phase you must push the problem into your subconscious mind. Forget it, get it completely out of your conscious mind and into your subconscious mind. When it tries to surface as the same old problem without a solution, push it back down and turn to something else.

After your mind has had a chance to come up with a solution—Ah-Ha! One day it will come to you. It may be in your sleep, as you are walking to work, or any number of other strange places.

Incubation is a problem-solving technique used by many creative problem-solvers. It is the same thing as the Ah-Ha principle but it is more universal. Incubation allows you to solve problems you aren't really worried about or consciously attempting to solve. It allows your mind to search out and solve problems that you may not have even recognized as problems.

Many of the great discoveries of our time have come about by mistakes. Scientists were working on problems that didn't pertain to the great discoveries at all.

The great secret to incubation is to write ideas down. When a novel thought strikes your mind, WRITE IT DOWN, so that you can ponder and think about it more in depth later on.

How many times have you had good ideas come to you that you couldn't remember later on? When you try to recall the "idea," you can't. But if you had written the thought down, you may have had the chance to develop a really revolutionary idea by thinking about it more in depth at a later date.

Ideas may come to you in your sleep. If they do, you can be reasonably sure if you don't write them down that by morning you won't be able to recall anything in enough detail. Carry a piece of paper with you. You might be tremendously surprised at how many good ideas pass you by regularly that you never catch and stop long enough to develop. Everyone has good ideas; it's just that most don't know how to recognize and develop the ideas that they have. Writing things down and allowing your mind to INCUBATE them will help tremendously. 18

"Fortune favors the prepared mind."
Louis Pasteur

PRO JEC TION

Have you ever seen a movie of yourself or heard your voice on a tape recorder? You probably didn't sound or act like you thought you did—proof again that you see things in your own unique way.

A mother once told an interesting story of how she began to see the world her little children saw. She was Christmas shopping with her little boy in New York City. The place was jammed with rushing shoppers, it had been raining, she still had many things to do and her young son was unhappy and complaining. While she was fighting the crowd through an aisle of a store, her son managed to convey to her that his shoe was untied and he was tripping on the lace.

In order to solve a design problem for someone or something other than yourself, it will help to change your point of view. Become the other person or object for a while. Stand in his shoes.

Projection is learning to see problems from the point of view which will give the best solution to the problem. There is a little saying which goes . . . What a Tiger eats becomes a Tiger and what a Lion eats becomes a Lion. In much the same way, what a designer sees becomes the design solution. The trick, then, is to see the things that will give the best solution to a particular problem.

She put her packages on the counter and squatted down to tie his shoe. As she did so, she suddenly saw the picture from his level. He was too small to see the display cases with their colorful items and lights. All he could see were legs, a wet and dirty floor, and big people charging at him from every direction. No wonder he was unhappy; there was nothing interesting or pleasant from his viewpoint.

She picked him up and carried him while she finished her shopping, and quickly headed for home.

116

Let's play a game that helps us to understand ourselves and others better. Imagine you are looking at yourself. You are sitting in a chair studying/Now take a closer look and see inside yourself. See your mind working, trying to understand the thing you are studying/See the little flashes of energy as you think hard/See your muscles move as you change positions/Feel the tenseness as you read something that you don't believe. You have many goals, fears, emotions, hangups that cause you to think in certain ways. Look at some of those goals and emotions. See something about yourself that you dislike. Don't be alarmed. Everyone has fears or feels disgust with himself. Don't judge yourself, just learn and understand yourself better.

Hopefully that little exercise helped you to realize something about yourself. What you should learn from it is that everyone has fears and emotions and hangups that direct his behavior. You see things differently than anyone else. You see things through your eyes screened by your goals, emotions, knowledge and hangups.

One secret to good design is the ability to see things from someone else's point of view. The more you can accept your internal feelings which prejudice your thinking and the better you can understand what those internal feelings are, the more easily you will be able to set feelings aside and see problems from other points of view.

Projection is the practice of seeing problems not from within, but from the correct perspective. Live the life of another for a short period of time and play the role which puts you in the middle of his problem to be solved.

Put yourself in someone else's shoes.

Jump in.

Put yourself into your chosen activity. See your world, and that around you, from the outside in and the inside out.

Everyone sees the world from a different view and it is essential that the designer learns to empathize with others so that he can solve their problems as well as his own.

Let's assume that you were asked to help design the layout of a building so that the blind would feel comfortable there. Would you find it helpful to blindfold yourself for one day and live within that building? Would you find it helpful to follow around a blind person and see the obstacles he encountered in the building?

Assume that you were asked to design a brochure for the elderly. You had a great deal of information to convey and the cost was tight so you designed it in 4 point type.

This brochure had a great deal of pertinent information and you were bewildered why it wasn't read by very many elderly. After all, it was a brochure directed to them with a title that let them know exactly that the information benefited them. Just because the type was so small that they couldn't easily read it was no excuse. Your eyes were good enough and you could see it and that was good enough.

Put yourself in other people's shoes for a while. You will be surprised at the improvement over your entire thinking.

As a designer, you may often be asked to solve problems relating to inanimate objects. You may need to design an easier rolling wheel for example. This same practice of placing yourself in the situation of the other person (in this case the ball bearing for that wheel) works well with objects also. By imagining yourself as a ball-bearing which helps that wheel roll more easily, you can design better. Feel the wheel grinding on you as it rotates. Feel the comfortable feeling of good lubrication reducing the friction. Feel the comfort when a few more ball bearings are placed next to you to help lighten your load. Feel the wheel turn easier or harder when different solutions are tried. Feel all of these things in your mind.

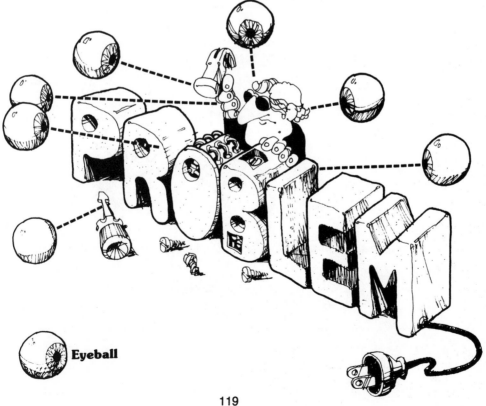

Eyeball

119

Synectics

William Gordon invented synectics here. Al Capp's cartoon shows a good example of how it works.

All too often we find ourselves looking at problems in the same old ways over and over again. Synectics is a method which helps us to look at a problem in completely different and creative ways time after time.

Synectics is highly successful and many of the world's greatest thinkers have used Synectics to help them solve their problems. They didn't call the method they used "Synectics" but the process they used was the same.

If the Synectics Process is to help us look at problems in different and creative ways, how is it done? Very simple! Synectics makes the strange seem familiar and the familiar seem strange. By doing this, synectics becomes a conscious attempt to achieve a new look at the same old world, people, ideas, feelings, and things.

Making the familiar strange → **Connection breaking** → **Making the strange familiar** → **Connection making** → (cycle)

MAKING THE FAMILIAR SEEM STRANGE

To make the familiar strange is to distort, invert, twist, transpose or in some other way change the manner in which we might normally look at problems. This pursuit of strangeness is not a meaningless search for the bizarre and out-of-the-ordinary, but it is a conscious attempt to achieve a new look at things. In the "familiar world" objects are always right-side-up (the child who bends and peers at the world from between his legs is experimenting with the familiar made strange).

All problems present themselves to the mind as threats of failure. This sometimes makes it difficult for someone to attempt to make the familiar seem strange. Our natural reaction would be to make the problem as familiar as we can, thereby relieving the threat of failure that the unknown creates. The concept of synectics however, is to make this problem seem even more strange and disorderly for a short period of time. From this approach, which causes temporary ambiguity and disorder, our mind is allowed to be more creative and free in solving the problem.

Synectics research utilizes four methods to make the familiar seem strange:

1. Personal Analogy
2. Direct Analogy
3. Symbolic Analogy
4. Fantasy Analogy

According to research, without the presence of these mechanisms no problem-stating, problem-solving attempt will be successful. These four methods are specific and reproducible mental processes, tools to initiate the creative mental process and to sustain and renew that process.

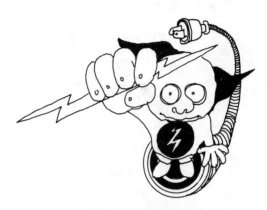

Become Electricity racing down the wire.

PERSONAL ANALOGY

Putting yourself into the problem is the first method of the problem-solving process. Usually a person will make a problem familiar to himself by stating it in terms or equations which he can manipulate. A chemist makes a problem familiar by looking at it in the form of mathematics, molecules and equations. If he were to permit himself to become a part of the problem by thinking himself to be a molecule and actually involved from a participating point of view, he would realize a completely different insight. By allowing himself to be a dancing molecule, pushed and pulled by the molecular forces, he feels what happens to a molecule. He remains a human being, but acts in his mind as though he were a molecule.

The personal analogy method of problem-solving is not a new process, but a long used creative problem-solving technique. Farady . . . "looked . . . into the very heart of the electrolyte endeavoring to render the play of its atom visable to his mental eyes" (Tyndall, 1968, pp. 66-67). Einstein recognized the role of personal analogy and even with the abstract area of mathematical thought identified "muscular" involvement.

In both science and art, detached observations and analysis are sometimes abandoned by great thinkers in favor of Personal Analogy.

Put yourself in the problem. Be a humming bird.

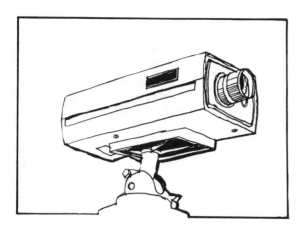

DIRECT ANALOGY

This mental process compares parallel facts to solve similar problems. For example: Sir March Isumbard Brunel solved the problem of underwater construction by watching a shipworm tunneling into a timber. The worm constructed a tube for itself as it moved forward, and the notion of caissons came to Brunel by direct analogy. Alexander Graham Bell recalled, "It struck me that the bones of the human ear were very massive, indeed, as compared with the delicate thin membrane that operated them, and the thought occurred that if a membrane so delicate could move bones relatively so massive, why should not a thicker and stouter piece of membrane move my piece of steel. Thus the telephone was conceived" (MacKenzie, 1928, pp. 72).

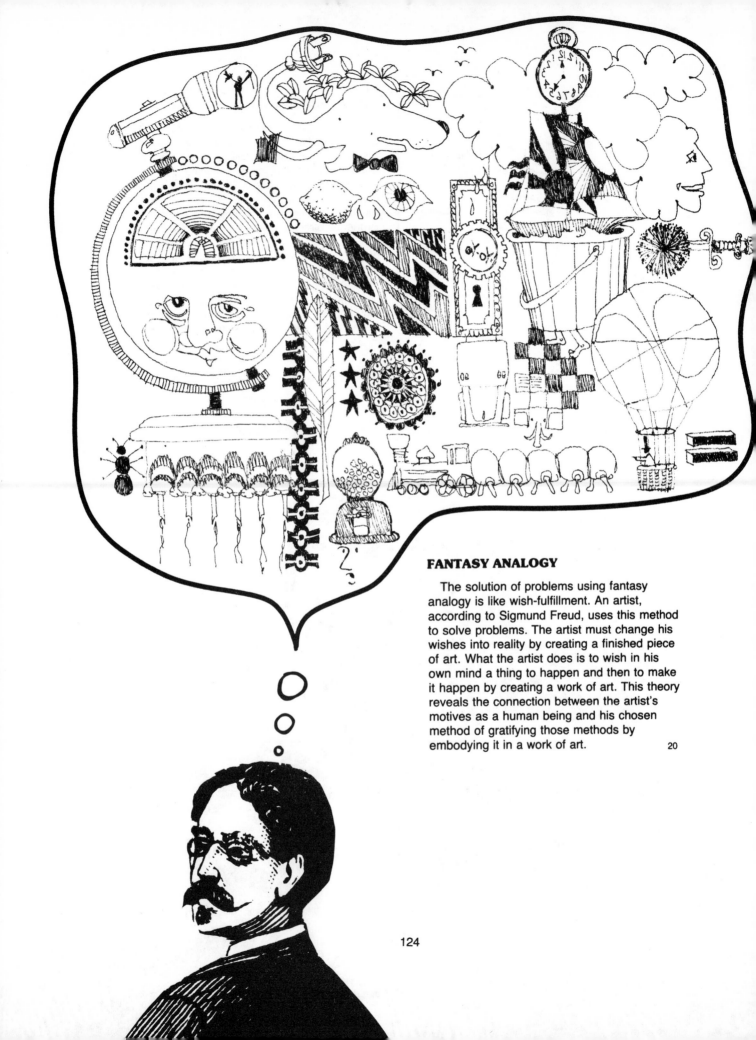

FANTASY ANALOGY

The solution of problems using fantasy analogy is like wish-fulfillment. An artist, according to Sigmund Freud, uses this method to solve problems. The artist must change his wishes into reality by creating a finished piece of art. What the artist does is to wish in his own mind a thing to happen and then to make it happen by creating a work of art. This theory reveals the connection between the artist's motives as a human being and his chosen method of gratifying those methods by embodying it in a work of art. 20

124

IT WOULD SEEM QUITE APPARENT THAT THERE IS NO ONE CREATIVE PROCESS AND THERE MAY WELL BE AS MANY CREATIVE PROCESSES AS THERE ARE CREATIVE PEOPLE

H. Herbert Fox

Bionics

Bionics—applying nature to man-made things.

Bionics is the use in nature of special devices found on both plants and animals to solve the special survival problems of the living creatures. Man, by adaptation, can use the same or similar principles to solve special design problems confronting him.

For some unknown reason, man has had a tendency throughout time to solve problems in his own way—not willing to learn from nature. When humans begin to take the marvelous creations of nature more seriously, our ability to solve problems will undoubtedly increase tremendously.

The marvelous designs of nature hold countless lessons to teach. To survive, each animal, insect, and plant has been forced to contrive actions, solutions, and designs that provide protective housing, that enhance the ability of sensing and capturing food, and that locate either prey or predator. Many of these designs are ingenious, and a large number are astonishingly beautiful. Many are simple designs. Others are quite complex. Whether ingenious, beautiful, simple or complex, all have one thing in common—they function extremely efficiently.

It is unfortunate that most often man has acted only as a casual observer of these ingenious designs of nature. More rarely, he has been a user of the products of nature's designs (such as diatomacious earth, spider-web threads and bamboo). Least frequently, he has been an imitator of nature and been able to make use of the unique solutions that nature has made available to us (such as flying machines, honeycomb structures, and poison arrows). In fact, in the majority of cases man has discovered the existence of some unique design in nature only after he himself had invented a similar device and learned to recognize its qualities. Examples are sonar and electric-field detection.

THE RADAR OF BATS

Long before man had heard of radar, bats were using it to navigate and locate their prey. They can fly at high speeds in total darkness, capturing flying insects and missing solid objects, demonstrating uncanny ability. They do so by giving off a series of ultrasonic cries and locating objects by the distance and direction of the sources and echoes.

A great deal of interest has been generated

in the bat's "radar" system because of two of its characteristics that are as yet unexplained. Some bats are able to locate fish beneath the surface of the water and it is not understood how this is done. Also, attempts to "jam" the bat's system with loud sound intensities have not been successful. In some way the bat is able to detect its own signal through a cacophony of sound.

HYPODERMIC FANGS

A little-comforting fact is that the modern hypodermic needle is patterned after the fang of a rattlesnake. A hollow tube in the fang of the snake allows poison to be injected beneath the perforated skin of its victim. This same principle allows medicinal serums to be injected beneath the skin of patients.

DEPTH CONTROL OF FISH

For millions of years fish have used a swim bladder which inflates or deflates with gas to help them maintain a desired depth in the water. This same principle is used by submarines to maintain certain depth levels in the ocean.

JET PROPULSION

One of the most modern and ingenious designs of man—the jet engine—has its antecedent in ancient designs of nature. The squid used jet propulsion to propel itself through the water. Fluid is forced out a funnel-shaped organ causing the creature to move forward.

Immature forms of dragonflies also employ jet propulsion for locomotion. These nymphs live in the water for 2 or 3 years before changing into the more familiar form of dragonflies. While in the water, the nymphs breathe by means of gills located in a cavity at the posterior end of the intestine. When the size of the cavity is increased, water enters. When the muscular walls of the cavity contract, water is forced out the posterior end of the animal and the nymph is forced forward. As a result the nymph moves in a sequence of short spurts.

LIGHT METERS

Modern automatic focus and exposure control cameras are patterned after the human eye. They operate on much the same principle as the iris in the human eye which opens and closes to control the amount of light allowed to enter the eye. The lens is shaped after the lens in the eye.

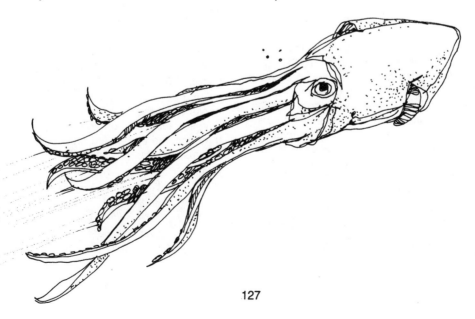

127

HEATING AND COOLING

Have you ever wondered why jackrabbits (a common sight in many western states) have such large ears? It isn't to hear better. Their ears actually act as coolers to dissipate heat build-up in their bodies. Laced with many blood vessels, the ears help dissipate heat as the animal holds its large ears errect while resting in the shade of a bush.

At the other end of the temperature scale, arctic seals can frequently be seen basking in the sun, sticking one flipper up into the sunshine. The flipper has a large surface area and is supplied abundantly with blood vessels. Heat is absorbed into the blood stream and carried throughout the body of the animal, thereby providing a localized source of heat for the animal.

Mallee fowl construct compost piles to provide heat for egg incubation. The female mallee lays eggs in a compost mound which the male builds, and maintains until the eggs hatch. He is able to keep the mound between 90° and 92°F. He does this by testing the mound with his beak—if it's too cold he adds more soil to the mound to maintain the heat produced by the decomposing plant materials. During time when the sun provides heat, the size of mound is reduced to allow the solar heat to warm the soils and eggs.

Man might someday use the techniques employed by the mallee fowl to better utilize the extremely vast resources of the sun and natural decomposition to provide heat for himself.

VISUAL CONCEALMENT

Camouflage, the art of concealment, has been developed to a science by the armed forces of almost every country. Similar techniques have been the basis for the survival of living organisms ever since life began.

LIGHT

Nearly everyone has seen fireflies and has marveled at their ability to produce light. The emission of light by organisms is called bioluminescence and is the result of an enzyme-catalyzed chemical reaction. While the usual incandescent lamp wastes 98% of the energy supplied, the efficiency of the cold-light production plant of the firefly is nearly 100% effective.

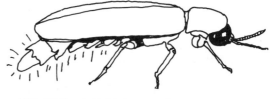

VELCRO—A MODERN FASTENER

Everyone who's ever strolled through country fields is familiar with the clinging burdock burr. But it took Swiss engineer George de Mestral's intense curiosity to really look into it and discover under microscope, how its tiny tenacious hooks could grab on to virtually any thread of hair, and not let go. After eight years and countless experiments, the VELCRO fastener was devised employing two mating nylon tapes. One section is covered with little hooks while the other section is covered with tiny, soft loops. When you press them together they become embedded and hold on with astonishing strength until you "peel" them apart.

Examples of modern bionic research

A study that has become a classic is the work of Lettvin, et al., at MIT on the eye of the frog. In operation, the frog's eye performs separate functions and screens out unwanted information. The eye responds only to moving objects against a background. Knowledge of how the frog is able to screen information could eventually lead to highly selective receiving apparatus. As an example, an experimental machine has been created which is able to distinguish targets from background noise on a radar screen.

One device developed by early bionics research is a ground speed-altitude indicator for aircraft based on the way the eye of a beetle functions. Research determined that the beetle distinguishes speed and altitude by "seeing" shadows pass by him. This same principle is utilized by aircraft which have a photo-cell mounted on the nose and tail of the plane. Measurements of the varying degrees of light and shadow which strike the photo-cells in sequence enable the plane's complex electrical system to determine speed.

A moth's ear is being studied to determine how two cells are able to screen and perceive the hostile sounds of an approaching bat which is the moth's predator.

Rattlesnakes are being studied to determine how they can perceive slight temperature changes. It has been learned that the reptiles can distinguish up to 0.001 centigrade change in body tissue temperature.

Birds are being studied in efforts to determine how they are able to navigate so effectively. Migration routes have intrigued man for some time now.

Several varieties of fish which have electro-receptors are being studied. The sensitivity of some of these animals is adequate enough to detect the lines of force in the earth's magnetic field when the fish is swimming at a rate of 0.25 feet per second. Some fish will respond to a comb run through the hair and placed in front of their tank. They can distinguish between conductors and nonconductors, or respond to a permanent magnet outside their tank.

"If no way be better than another— that, you may be sure, is Nature's way."
Leibniz

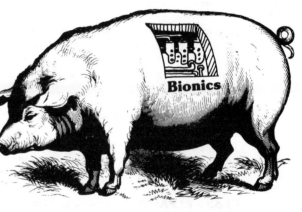

"In the works of Nature, purpose not accident, is the main thing."
Aristotle

Pag Pau

Attempts at manipulating creative thinking which resulted in synectics groups also produced a thought process for arriving at creative solutions to problems. This thought process we'll call **PAG PAU**. **PAG** means **P**roblem **A**s **G**iven and **PAU** means **P**roblem **A**s **U**nderstood.

The following is a flow chart of the general thought processes which have been observed to occur during the creative solution of a problem:

Problem as Given—Analysis and Explanation by an Expert
Problem is presented.

An expert in the area of the problem is consulted in an attempt to better understand the problem.

Purge—Brainstorming Session with an Expert

With the expert present, a brainstorming session is conducted. The expert explains why some of the suggested solutions will or will not work. This helps one to better understand the problem.

Problem as Understood

The creative problem-solving participants are asked to write goals or possible problems which he sees that need to be solved.

Choice of PAU Evocative Question

A goal is chosen—the creative process begins to find solutions. A question is posed which demands use of one of the 4 analogical responses. This continues until some other analogies have been explored. It is concluded by summarizing the best analogies into short sentences—as though it were a book title for the analogy.

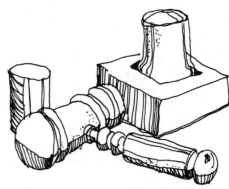

Make an idea fit another context.

Force Fit

Although the analogical mechanisms lie at the heart of the synectics method, they must be "force-fitted" to the problem if they are to be effective. The chosen analogies are stretched and pulled and refocused in order that they might become solutions to the problem at hand.

Viewpoint

A choice of the force-fitted analogies which might prove to be useable solutions is made. This is equivalent to a conclusion to any of the solutions which prove to be at all worthwhile.

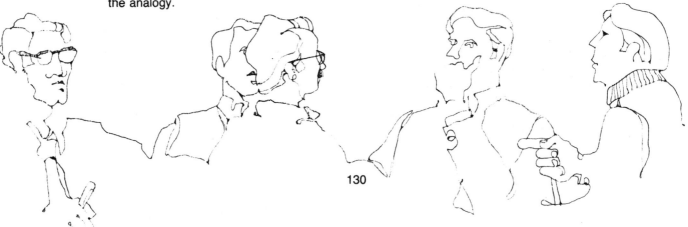

130

A Typical Session

PAG: How we determine oil saturation in reservoir rock.

Analysis Expert: "In wells we are drilling now we have a serious problem of getting a representative sample of the reservoir rock. The best method so far is to put down a hollow bit on the drill pipe and cut a core. We bring up this sample of the reservoir rock and then try to guess how representative it is. Trouble is that we may have 300 psi pressure at the reservoir. As we bring the core up through six or seven thousand feet of muddy water this pressure is released—that and sloshing around in the muddy water makes a big difference between the core we have to examine and the reservoir. If we had accurate data on oil saturation, we could calculate the reserves, get better information on our recovery percentages. It would really do us a lot of good."

Purges: None

PAU'S:

1. How to make reservoir rock tell us the truth.

2. How to have oil tell me how crowded it is in the reservoir rock.

LEADER: Number 2 has a look of appeal. Now please put the problem out of your mind.

Evocative question: Example
LEADER: My Evocative Question is for an example from biology of a crowded situation.

TOM: I don't mean it to be facetious but flies on a cow flop.
LEADER: Yes?
TOM: Well, it's a crowded situation . . . I mean those flies are two or three deep on there.
BOB: Ant hill.
HARRY: Virus culture.
LEADER: Say more about virus culture.
HARRY: It is a funny kind of crowd. It might start out very thin, but it multiplies and makes itself into a crowd.
LEADER: Do you mean it is sort of dedicated to making a crowd of itself?
HARRY: Partly that, but I was thinking that it has a deadly intention and needs a crowd to win.
TOM: Womb with triplets.
DICK: Drop of sperm.
HARRY: Seedling.
LEADER: Let's take this virus culture. Now take a couple of minutes . . . don't say anything while you get into your new skin . . . You are one virus in this culture . . . How do you feel?
Leader writes: EQ:PA (Personal Analogy), Virus Culture. (He waits.)
BOB: I am very small but so is everyone else. I am curled like a corkscrew.
LEADER: Anyone feel differently?
DICK: It's nice and warm in this culture, but I feel itchy . . . I am dissatisfied . . . because I want to go out on my own . . . These guys are too self-satisfied and smug for me . . . I'm going for a sensitive spot where I can set up my own culture.
TOM: I feel a sense of real urgency . . . panic because I keep turning into two of me and then four . . . and everyone else is doing it . . . I can feel the food getting hard to get . . . got to die . . . want to do something fast but nothing to do—except multiply. My only mission.
LEADER: Your only mission? Who sent you on your mission? (Pause).
TOM: Fate . . . no, not really fate, it was evolution. I wasn't always this way . . . this prolific and deadly. I have evolved . . . you know . . . natural selection—man, I have ancestors who came over on the Mayflower.
LEADER: Great! Does anyone feel differently about being a virus?
BOB: I hate the world. I want to get into some other place—out of this culture where I can kill other things alive. It's a black world . . . I want to murder.
HARRY: I feel I am a very successful virus. With the way these other guys feel I can sit back and relax, enjoy life and play a guitar. One is going to take care of the reproducing and killing. Why should I worry?
TOM: I resent his playing his guitar while I'm panicky.

LEADER: This is a rich haul . . . Now my Evocative Question is for a Book Title. Can you give me a two word title—poetic and compelling that captures the essence of virus culture and contains a paradox?
Leader writes: EQ:BT for Virus Culture. (Long Silence)
LEADER: How about Dick's idea of "warm" and Bob's murderous feelings. Can we make something of that?
DICK: How about warm hate?
LEADER: The paradox is there, but I miss the essence. Say what you were thinking.
DICK: I just picked my "warm" and substituted hate for murder, but I guess a virus doesn't bother with hate.
TOM: Indifferent destruction.

131

LEADER: You got some of the essence. Can we improve on "indifferent" so the words fight more?
HARRY: How about affectionate destruction?
LEADER: Neat!
BOB: Indifferent purposefulness.
LEADER: What are you thinking?
BOB: From Tom's idea, the virus couldn't care less about his host, but he has a strong sense of purpose. Like Dick said in his Personal Analogy . . . he's ambitious and wants to grow and multiply.
DICK: Compulsive indifference.
LEADER: Let's go with that. My Evocative Question is for an Example from nature of compulsive indifference. (EQ:EX)
DICK: Queen bee.
LEADER: Say more about this Queen bee.
DICK: Well I was thinking of their mating . . . She has the compulsion, but she flies away from the males . . . higher and higher . . . When one of the males finally mates with her, she is indifferent enough to kill him.
LEADER: Do you mean the way she plays hard to get . . . the flying high and then when she does let a male make it . . . killing—is a mixture of compulsion and indifference?
DICK: Yeah.
TOM: Cat.
LEADER: Yes?
TOM: A cat has compulsive curiosity, for instance, and yet the cats I know are quite indifferent to their owner.
LEADER: If I get you, this is a strange combination in cats; being curious implies interest, even concern . . . yet a cat doesn't give a damn about her best friend—her owner.
TOM: Yes, cats are a queer combination.
LEADER: Let's examine a cat. I've spent a lot of time wondering about them. Tom, tell us more about cats.
TOM: It seems to me that each tomcat has a territory. He chases out the other toms and keeps the females for himself.
HARRY: We had a big tom once, and he had a huge territory—several square blocks. He'd come stumbling home each morning with pieces chewed out of him. My 5-year-old son who owned him said to him one morning, "Sniffer, is it worth it?"
DICK: You know the way cats lie perfectly still and relaxed. Every once in a while the tip of their tails flip as though to warn anyone, "I'm alert, baby!"
TOM: Cats can be responsive though; you pat or stroke them and gradually they'll relax and purr.

132

Forcing something from something else

DICK: I think of cats as loners. They don't travel around in packs like dogs.
LEADER: Let's move into Force Fit. How can we take this idea of cat and use it to help us have the oil tell us how crowded in the reservoir rock it is?
DICK: Something comes to me. If a cat gets crowded he loses all his indifference . . . He gets into a rage.
LEADER: You mean, we might crowd the oil a little in some way and then it would yell and tell us how crowded . . .
TOM: I think I have a viewpoint.
LEADER: Are you going to build on Dick's?
TOM: Well, no, it's different.
LEADER: Please make a note; we'll come back to you. Is there some way we can put this oil in a rage so it . . .
BOB (THE EXPERT): If you take the pressure off it becomes a rage. It boils and fumes and carries on. But you would like it . . . calm. You want to talk to it while it is not a rage, because then it is oil-like. It's got the essence of a cat . . . You don't want to talk to the cat when he is in a rage . . . he's not communicating.
LEADER: How can we calm the oil down?
HARRY: Stroke it!
LEADER: OK, let's stroke it. What does it mean to stroke that oil?
HARRY: You stroke it just like a cat, and it calms down . . . maybe it purrs. You stroke that oil.
BOB (EXPERT MUSINGLY): Yeah, you got to stroke that oil.
TOM: It even arches its back as you stroke it. It will react to your stroking.
BOB (SOFTLY): Chill it . . . cool it down.
LEADER: If you want, we'll freeze it. Pump liquid . . . what is that stuff?
BOB: Nitrogen! By God, maybe that's it . . . We pump down liquid nitrogen and freeze the hell out of that formation.
LEADER: We're with you . . .
BOB: We'll freeze the water and the oil and everything and core right into it. Everything will stay right put.
HARRY: Petrified candy!
BOB: We'll drill some and keep it cold some way. We'll freeze it and keep it cold as we bring it up . . . We just might have something.

In the Expert's view this was a new and worthwhile way to view the problem, and it was written up as a Viewpoint.   21

133

Change

A designer is a change agent. He deals with change, manipulates it, profits by it, and learns from it. He helps others to be comfortable in a changing world.

Since change is such an important part of the design profession, a look at the past will help build appreciation for the ever-changing present and future.

Have you ever talked with your grandfather about his younger days? His transportation likely was dominated by early automobiles. He never dreamed of airplanes becoming such a major part of life. Income tax was only about 1% then. Sixty-hour work weeks were standard. Wages were 30¢ per hour and inflation was about non-existent. Cars were few, highways non-existent, traffic problems undreamed of, and electricity fairly new.

In looking at the past and contemplating the future, it makes you wonder how people can become bored, doesn't it? To a designer, the future and change hold promise of fun, fame and fortune.

Take a minute and imagine some of the possibilities ahead. Think of some of the ways a designer will be required to solve tomorrow's needs. Think of some of the new designer possibilities ahead in the fields of:

Architecture
Television
Ground Transportation
Air Travel
Medical Devices
Interiors
Clothes
Furniture
Communications
Graphics

And on and on and on . . .

134

It's almost frightening to try to imagine what tomorrow will bring. It's for sure a creative and informed designer—no matter what his field of emphasis—has a bright future ahead.

Just to help emphasize the thousands of things that come and go year by year, do you remember: Hula hoops, frisbies, passenger trains, Gant shirts, fruit loops, white socks, stretch Levi's, leather jackets and greasy hair, the crew cut, Wolfman Jack, rock 'n' roll, '57 Chevies, 45 records, fizzies, Maypo, The Mickey Mouse Club, Batman, Laugh-in, a 30¢ gallon of gas, Watergate, the bionic man, or today's news?

A designer has the responsibility to perpetuate good from the past and present and to improve the bad. The designer has a bright future, a responsibility to improve himself and his environment, and a tomorrow that promises excitement.

There is nothing quite as sure as change!

DO IT!

The young man had captured a small bird which he held tightly in his hand. "Now is my chance," he thought, "to learn just how smart the wise old man of the village really is."

"I'll ask the old man whether the bird I hold concealed in my hand is alive or dead," he thought to himself as he hurried across the village square to the dwelling of the wise old man. "If he replies 'It is dead,' then I'll open my hands and allow it to fly away. And if he says 'It is alive,' then I shall squeeze my hand tightly and crush the bird for him to see."

The walk to the wise man's house took but a few minutes. The boy tightly held the frightened, quiet bird in his lethal grasp. Upon arriving at the house, he summoned the wise man to help him solve a complex problem.

"I hold a bird tightly in my grasp behind my back," he said to the wise man of the village. "I want you, who seems to know everything, to tell me whether it is alive or it is dead."

The wise man looked directly into the questioning eyes of the small boy and firmly replied, "IT IS UP TO YOU!"

Isn't life that way with us? Isn't it up to us? Don't we hold our own fate within our own grasp?

You probably haven't heard of the greatest designer that ever lived. Alvort Schwartz was his name. He was one of the smartest, most creative, capable designer-inventor who ever lived. He had more POTENTIAL than probably anyone who has lived in the last 100 years. Unfortunately very few people have ever heard of the great Alvort Schwartz. You see, Alvort Schwartz never did anything. Unlike Edison, Bell, Pasteur, Ford, and Einstein, Alvort Schwartz wasted his talented potential by doing nothing. So instead of being the greatest designer-inventor of our century, Alvort Schwartz was the greatest mistake. He was the greatest waste. He chose to be 'lifeless' when he could have been 'alive.'

Many talented and intelligent people spend their efforts proclaiming excellence and doing very little.

Mark Twain once pointed out that "Noise proves nothing. Often a hen who has merely laid an egg cackles as if she had laid an asteroid."

No matter what people say or how much they boast or what potential they have, THEY ARE BUT WHAT THEY ARE (as demonstrated by what they accomplish with their talents).

For every idea carried to fruition, there are probably a million good ideas that people think of but don't do anything about. Many designers and inventors worry about someone stealing their "GREAT IDEAS." They probably should worry more about doing something with them. The greatest stealer of good ideas is the "do-nothing man"—that demon who lets ideas waste in the mind of the lazy person.

Theodore Roosevelt, who led the "rough riders," was born a weak and sickly child. Demosthenes, who became the greatest orator in the world, started out with a paralyzing speech defect. Beethoven was deaf, John Milton blind, and Julius Caesar an epileptic. Lincoln lacked schooling and was awkward and ungainly. But each in his own field turned weaknesses into strengths.

Creation did not go to all the trouble involved in organizing the universe and placing us in the center of it with the thought we should waste our lives.

For every person with a spark of genius, there are a hundred with ignition trouble.

Many of us have the right aim in life. We just never get around to pulling the trigger.

And for you who read these pages and think you can't do it—that's a bunch of bunk. You'll never know until you try. Even if you try and fail, you still may not have the justification to quit—some of the greatest accomplishments of all time have come from weak and nearly handicapped people who wouldn't quit.

DO IT! DESIGN!

Acknowledgments

1. Chrysler Motors Co.
2. Pacific Telephone, Larry Stropes, BBDO Advertising
3. *Industrial Design,* Harold Van Doren, McGraw Hill
4. Braun
5. Eastman Kodak Company
6. Smith-Corona Corp.
7. *The Measure of Man: Human Factors in Design,* Henry Dreyfuss, MIT Press
8. Herman Miller
9. The Mero System, Wurzburg, Germany
10. *The Meaning of Meaning,* O.K. Ogden and I.A. Richards, Harcourt Brace Jovanovich, Inc.
11. *Psycho-Cybernetics,* Maxwell Maltz, Wilshire.
    Our Changing World, Earl Nightingale, Nightingale-Covant Corp.
12. Bernard M. Patten, M.D.
14. *Experiences in Visual Thinking,* Robert McKim, Brooks/Cole Publishing Co.
    Put Your Mother on the Ceiling, Richard deMille, Viking Press
15. *The Universal Traveler,* Don Koberg and Jim Bagnall, William Kaufmann, Inc.
16. *Applied Imagination,* Alex Osborn, Scribners
17. Creative Education Foundation, State University of New York at Buffalo
    Design Methods, J.C. Jones, Wiley
    Conceptual Blockbusting, James L. Adams, W.H. Freeman and Co.
18. *Our Changing World,* Earl Nightingale, Nightingale-Covant Corp.
19. Al Capp, Fortune Magazine
20. *The Metaphorical Way,* William Gordon, Porpoise Books
21. *Synectics*, William Gordon, Harper and Row

References

Picture it in your mind's eye

The Universal Traveler, Don Koberg and Jim Bagnall, William Kaufmann, Inc.

Put Your Mother on the Ceiling, Richard de de Mille, Viking Press

Communication Probes, Brent D. Peterson, Science Research Associates

The Meaning of Meaning, O.K. Ogden and I.A. Richards, Harcourt Brace Jovanovich, Inc.

Psycho-Cybernetics, Maxwell Maltz, Wilshire

Designing for People, Henry Dreyfuss, Viking Press

Survival Through Design, Richard Neutra, Oxford University Press

Good or Bad Design?, Odd Brochmann, Van Nostrand Reinholt

Values Tech., Don Koberg and Jim Bagnall, William Kaufmann, Inc.

Introduction to Engineering, Design and Graphics, George C. Blakley and Ernest G. Chilton, The Macmillian Co.

Drawing as a Means to Architecture, William K. Lockard, Van Nostrand Reinhold Co.

Training Creative Thinking, Gary A. Davis and Joseph A. Scott, Holt, Rinehart and Winston, Inc.

Conceptual Blockbusting, James L. Adams, W.H. Freeman and Co.

Design with Nature, Ian McHarg, Natural History Press

Self-Renewal, John W. Gardner, Harper and Row

Design Methods, J.C. Jones, Wiley

The Metaphorical Way, William Gordon, Porpoise Books

Synectics, William Gordon, Harper and Row

Notes on the Synthesis of Form, C. Alexander, Harvard University Press

Experiences in Visual Thinking, Robert McKim, Brooks/Cole Publishing Co.

The Language of Drawing, Edward Hill, Prentice Hall

On Knowing: Essays for the Left Hand, Jerome Bruner, Belknap Press

Visual Thinking, Rudolph Arnheim, University of California Press

The Natural Way to Draw, Kimon Nicolaides, Houghton Mifflin

Perspectice: A New System for Designers, Jay Doblin, Whitney

Applied Imagination, Alex Osborn, Scribners

The Five-Day Course in Thinking, Edward DeBono, Pelican

New Think, Edward DeBono, Basic Books

On Creativity, Don Fabun, Glencoe Press

Index

About the Authors

KURT HANKS
works as a design consultant designing
Information Centers, Museums and Visitor
Centers. He teaches at Brigham Young
University in the Department of Art and Design
in the Industrial Design Program.

DAVE EDWARDS
owns Design Associates and teaches at
Brigham Young University. He teaches in the
Industrial Design Program and has done
design work primarily in the electronic and
energy conservation fields.

LARRY BELLISTON
is president of an information design firm in
Salt Lake City, Utah. He has worked in
advertising and public relations with his
principle activities centering around graphic arts
and mass media communication.

Notes

Notes

Notes